AUCTIONS

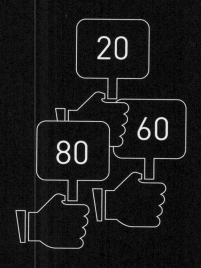

The MIT Press Essential Knowledge Series

AUCTIONS

TIMOTHY P. HUBBARD AND HARRY J. PAARSCH

The MIT Press | Cambridge, Massachusetts | London, England

MIT Press books may be purchased at special quantity discounts for business or sales promotional use. For information, please email special_sales@ mitpress.mit.edu.

Set in Chaparral Pro by the MIT Press. Printed and bound in the United States of America.

Library of Congress Cataloging-in-Publication Data

Hubbard, Timothy P., author.
Auctions / Timothy P. Hubbard and Harry J. Paarsch.
    pages   cm.—(The MIT Press essential knowledge series)
Includes bibliographical references and index.
ISBN 978-0-262-52853-5 (pbk. : alk. paper) 1. Auctions. I. Paarsch, Harry J.,
author. II. Title.
HF5476.H83   2015
381'.17—dc23

                                                          2015030655

10 9 8 7 6 5 4 3 2 1

Dedicated to my family

Dedicated to the memory of
Betty Johanna Maria Louise Haase Paarsch
February 6, 1923–May 2, 2009

CONTENTS

SERIES FOREWORD

The MIT Press Essential Knowledge series offers accessible, concise, beautifully produced pocket-size books on topics of current interest. Written by leading thinkers, the books in this series deliver expert overviews of subjects that range from the cultural and the historical to the scientific and the technical.

In today's era of instant information gratification, we have ready access to opinions, rationalizations, and superficial descriptions. Much harder to come by is the foundational knowledge that informs a principled understanding of the world. Essential Knowledge books fill that need. Synthesizing specialized subject matter for nonspecialists and engaging critical topics through fundamentals, each of these compact volumes offers readers a point of access to complex ideas.

Bruce Tidor
Professor of Biological Engineering and Computer Science
Massachusetts Institute of Technology

Auctions have been used since antiquity. For instance, the Roman Empire was once sold at auction. Today, auctions are seemingly pervasive: the institution is used to sell a variety of agricultural commodities and natural resources—from aubergine to tobacco, from fish to oil to timber—as well as fine art, real estate, and used cars. In addition sealed-bid tenders (an auction format) are used extensively by both firms and governments to procure a variety of goods and services such as weapons systems and tree-planting services. The Internet auction house eBay is an integral part of the American and world economies. By any measure, the volume of trade on eBay and similar sites is unparalleled in world history.

People around the world google thousands of times each second, the results of their requests appearing in the iconic results page—the organic results on the left and the advertised ones to the right, separated by merely a few whitespace characters. The order of those links on the right is determined at a position auction, a type of auction that has generated billions in revenues for Google. In short, it is impossible to live in the world today without being affected by auctions.

Despite the importance of auctions, except for a modest number of economists with special training, few understand beyond a simple level how these mechanisms really work. In fact most people are unaware that different auction formats and pricing rules even exist. To be sure, many books (search "eBay auctions" under Books on Amazon. com) provide concrete advice concerning how to buy or to sell on eBay. Others provide practical advice concerning how to sell real estate or to buy used cars at auctions. However useful these books may be, they do not explain when and why auctions work so well, or how. Several advanced textbooks, aimed mostly at graduate students and professional economists, have been written since 2000 documenting the progress economists have made in understanding purposeful, equilibrium behavior at auctions; for example, see the books by Vijay Krishna (2002, 2010), Paul Klemperer (2004), and Paul R. Milgrom (2004). But these books are really at levels beyond what most people can be reasonably expected to explore. The book by Kenneth Steiglitz (2007) is easy to read, but devoted mostly to eBay auctions. By writing this book, we hope to fill a niche, providing material that is straightforward to understand, yet rich enough to inform—in short, the essentials.

In chapter 1 we motivate the study of auctions by outlining what we consider an auction to be, describing commonly employed auctions and characterizing environments within which auctions are most helpful. Equipped with this overview, in chapter 2 we then turn our attention to modeling auctions. Economists consider auctions to be examples of games of asymmetric information—some players know something that other players do not. For example, at some auctions, each bidder might know what an item is worth to him but not how rivals value the item. The seller presumably knows even less: not only might the seller not know a particular bidder's valuation, he likely won't even know which bidder values the item the most. Adopting a baseline model, in chapter 3 we characterize equilibrium behavior under the common auction formats and pricing rules, discussing important properties of the outcomes at auctions. In chapter 4 we examine the implications of using other auction rules and different modeling assumptions, contrasting the outcomes with those of the benchmark model. We devote chapters 5 and 6 to deeper examinations of specific environments—procurement and Internet auctions, respectively. Such settings allow us to investigate the incentives at play at auctions that are important in modern economies. While the focus in the first six chapters is primarily on settings in which a single object is at auction, in chapter 7 we discuss auctions at which multiple units of the same good or several different objects are for sale, using online ad auctions in chapter 8 as an outlet for an in-depth discussion of some of the issues that arise in those settings. We reflect on what has been covered by collecting some final thoughts in chapter 9. At the end of the book we provide a glossary that collects important terms and definitions that may be helpful in reading the book and, in a separate section, list other resources that interested readers can use to learn more about auctions.

ACKNOWLEDGMENTS

Between us we have been studying auctions for a combined forty years. During these years we have received much helpful feedback from many cohorts of students. Several of our colleagues also provided us with concrete feedback concerning previous drafts of this book. We are especially grateful to our friend Srihari Govindan as well as four anonymous referees who read preliminary drafts of the manuscript and provided useful comments and helpful suggestions.

At the MIT Press Jane Macdonald was particularly efficient in putting together an attractive set of terms for us as well as guiding the project through the production process. We thank her for the expertise and professionalism. We also thank Emily Taber of the MIT Press for her careful reading of the penultimate manuscript and for providing editorial suggestions that forced us to be clear and improved our exposition.

AUCTION FORMATS AND PRICING RULES

Before proceeding with any analysis of bidding behavior at auctions, knowing what constitutes an auction is important. In this chapter we describe the most common four different types of auctions and then outline when it useful to use an auction, and why.

What's an Auction?

Ask anyone what they think of when they hear the word "auction" and you will get a variety of responses, some of them involving such terms as "antiques," "art," or "wine," but also "charity" and "silent." Many people associate images or construct visions when the word is heard— fast-talking auctioneers pointing in different directions, bidders raising and lowering paddles in succession, gavels being hammered down. For some, auctions represent elite, black-tie events attended by the wealthy. With such tangible associations it is no wonder the intricacies of how bidders behave and the design of alternative selling mechanisms are overlooked.

The descriptions of some auctions have imbued them with romantic qualities. After the reigning emperor had been overthrown in AD 193, the entire Roman Empire was sold at auction. When computer programmer Pierre Omidyar sold a broken laser pointer for more than $14 using his online company AuctionWeb, he surely had no idea his website, now eBay, would become a Fortune 500 company. Were he alive, the Norwegian artist Edvard Munch would probably be astonished to learn that his painting *The Scream* fetched nearly $120 million at auction.

Although these anecdotes may be inspirational, in other cases auctions generate controversy, even raise ethical issues. The Babylonians used auctions to sell wives. In the antebellum South of the United States, slaves were frequently sold at auction. More recently websites hosting so-called virginity auctions have been constructed. Auctions have earned notoriety in other ways as well. Suppliers of milk to public schools in several US states were found guilty of bid-rigging, resulting in a number of individuals having to pay fines and to serve time in prison. In 2000, executives at the world's two premier auction houses for high-quality art, Christie's and Sotheby's (both founded in London in the eighteenth century), were indicted with having conspired to fix the commission fees charged. For violating antitrust laws, fines were paid by and prison sentences were meted out to those found guilty.

With use dating back to at least 500 BC, the auction is among the oldest market institutions. That this institution is ancient does not mean it is obsolete. Rather, the durability of the selling mechanism signals its remarkable flexibility and robustness—its economic fitness. As selling mechanisms go, auctions are amazingly resilient. Moreover auctions are constantly being employed in novel ways. For example, music has been traditionally sold as a good intended to be enjoyed by the consumer who purchased the album. We are surely not the first to observe, however, that many listeners of a band's album likely have not purchased the music. Perhaps this is why the American hip-hop group Wu-Tang Clan announced in the summer of 2014 plans to sell at auction the only copy of their album *Once Upon A Time In Shaolin*. The winner of the auction will have full rights: he or she can keep the music for personal use only, hold private listening parties for others to attend, or release the album to the world at no cost.

Auctions drive the modern economy. In the Internet-based world, information gathered from your Facebook profile or from your browsing history is used by websites to garner higher prices from advertisers interested in targeting particular kinds of consumers. How? Using auctions, of course.

Before proceeding any further, however, it is worth asking: what is an auction? First and foremost, an auction is a way of allocating an object or acquiring a service. For the auction to work well, the rules determining the winner as well as how much that bidder will pay must be established beforehand. Moreover potential bidders must be made aware of these rules, and understand them. Most important, the auctioneer commits not to change any of the rules. The auctioneer is a middleman who collects information from the bidders in the form of bids that reflect their willingness to pay for the object on sale. How such information is gathered is part of the rules of the auction and must also be made known to the bidders *before* the auction. Having gathered the information, the auctioneer determines the winner using the agreed-on rules; the object (or service) is awarded to the winner and payment made to the seller (or his agent, the auctioneer, who need not be the seller) using the agreed-on pricing rule.

Although this description is incredibly general, the simplest way to think about an auction is, then, as a way of gathering information combined with formal allocation and pricing rules. No limit exists concerning what types of objects can be sold at auction: you will see auctions being used to sell many different commodities—electricity, fish, flowers, fruit, livestock, oil, timber, vegetables, wine, and wool as well as antique coins, financial securities, hotel rooms, old stamps, pollution permits, real estate, sports

First and foremost,
an auction is a way of
allocating an object or
acquiring a service.

memorabilia, and used cars. Famous authors have used auctions to sell the right to publish books from manuscripts; at some universities, opportunities for students to enroll in courses are allocated using auctions. Nothing really restricts the way in which information is gathered as bids can be submitted in arbitrary ways. A seller may ask the bidders to acknowledge whether they are willing to pay a certain asking price or to write down offers on paper. At the Tsukiji Market in Tokyo, bidders use hand signals to convey bids for fresh fish. Furthermore no regulations exist concerning the amount of time required to sell an object at auction. Filene's Basement was a discount retailer in Boston that automatically marked down all items by increasingly higher percentages over a thirty-day period before giving unsold items to charity. As will be clear soon, this can be thought of as a drawn-out Dutch auction. Traded prices can be determined in several different ways. As long as all parties are privy to the format (the way in which information is gathered by the seller or his agent, the auctioneer) and the rules (the timing of when the information must be submitted by the bidders, how the winner is determined, the rule determining the price that the winner must pay), we consider the market institution to be an auction.

Despite their durability and flexibility, auctions appear underappreciated, not just by the typical person, but also by many economists. Ask your closest acquaintance who majored in economics in college how much that person knows about auctions; the answer will be disappointing. In fact the word "auction" is scarcely even heard within the walls of economics classrooms around the world. If the word does appear in the typical economics curriculum, then it is likely in the context of a Walrasian auctioneer—a mystical being who is as real as Adam Smith's "invisible hand." This is unfortunate, especially since auctions have been, and continue to be, a consistently important feature of the global economic system. That auctions are seemingly absent from many undergraduate curricula is particularly disturbing because economic researchers of auctions have made arguably some of the most practical contributions to policy. For example, when policy makers around the world decided to sell off the rights to use the electromagnetic spectrum for such devices as cell phones, they turned to auction researchers to design markets that would both allocate the spectrum to the best possible use and generate billions of dollars in revenue for the respective governments. As a signal of the intellectual importance of auctions, several recipients of the Sveriges Riksbank Prize in Economic Sciences in Memory of Alfred Nobel (also known as the Nobel Prize in Economics) have been honored for their research of auctions—William S. Vickrey specifically, but Eric S. Maskin and Roger B. Myerson for their work in mechanism design, and Vernon L. Smith and Alvin E. Roth for their work concerning alternative market mechanisms too. Before developing an understanding of the significance of the work of these Nobel laureates, and other accomplished researchers as well, we first outline some commonly employed types of auctions.

Types of Auctions

Four types of auctions, and variants of them, make up the majority of auctions used in practice. Understanding these four types of auctions will provide you with a base from which to gain insight into a host of other types of auctions that you might encounter or imagine. In table 1 we describe these four types of auctions in terms of two useful partitions: first, the auction format; second, the pricing rule.

The two auction formats are the *open* (sometimes referred to as the *oral* or the *open outcry* format) and the *sealed-bid*, perhaps best thought of as the *closed* format.

Table 1 Types of auctions

		Pricing rule	
		First-price	Second-price
	Open	Dutch; oral, descending-price	English; oral, ascending-price
Auction format	**Sealed-bid**	Pay-your-bid; first-price, sealed-bid	Vickrey; second-price, sealed-bid

Two important pricing rules are used to determine what the winning bidder will pay. Under the first, the winner must pay what was bid; this is referred to as the *first-price* rule, at least by economists. Under the second, the winner must pay what the highest opponent bid (the second-highest bid), so this is referred to as the *second-price* rule. These two partitions yield four combinations of auction formats and pricing rules—four types of auctions. We begin by examining these four types of auctions.

Perhaps the best-known type of auction is the oral, ascending-price auction, which is sometimes referred to as the *English auction*. The word auction in fact derives from the Latin word *auctus*—the past participle of the verb *augere*, which means to augment or to raise. If you mention the word auction to someone, that person will probably think of an English auction. At an English auction the auctioneer begins by introducing an opening price and then asking the bidders whether they are willing to pay this price. If no bidder is willing to pay the opening price, then the auctioneer will often decrease the asking price until at least one bidder is willing to accept the asking price. Having obtained participation, the auctioneer will then call out a higher price. If no one is willing to pay the higher asking price, the bidder willing to pay the standing price is awarded the object at that price. If someone is willing to pay a higher asking price, then successively higher prices are called out by the auctioneer until only one bidder is willing to pay the standing price. At this point the object is then *knocked down* by the auctioneer and sold to the highest bidder. At some auctions, bidders may be permitted to cry out bids that exceed the current asking price, perhaps as a way to speed up the selling process, or even to try to intimidate rival bidders. The English auction is used by the world's two largest auction houses Christie's and Sotheby's to sell high-quality antiques, art, jewelry, and wine among other things. The auction house Barrett-Jackson employs the English auction to sell classic automobiles. The English auction is also used to sell abandoned property on the A&E reality television program *Storage Wars*. You will find English auctions being held in barns and churches as well as antique shops around the world.

In contrast to the oral, ascending price of the English auction is the oral, descending-price auction, often referred to as the *Dutch auction*, perhaps because this type of auction is used to sell flowers in the town of Aalsmeer in the Netherlands. Dutch auctions can involve an auctioneer who calls out successively lower prices, but often a clock is used to automate the task. Specifically, the clock is set at a very high price that represents the opening price for the object at auction. When the auction begins, the clock ticks down—the asking price descends. The first buyer to stop the clock, either by shouting "Stop!" or by using some other device, wins the auction and must pay the current price on the clock. Even though Dutch and English auctions are open formats, the incentives of bidders under the two pricing rules are different: at English auctions, the winner stops increasing bids when the last rival drops out and thus pays an amount that is linked to a competitor's bid, while at Dutch auctions the winner pays the highest (only) bid. Below, we will discuss how the ascending-/descending- and first-/second-price features affect bidder behavior. For now, it is sufficient to note that at English auctions many bids can be (and are often) made, so the bidding process can take some time, whereas at Dutch auctions only one bid is observed—that of the winner, who has stopped the price clock, indicating a willingness to pay that price. This distinction is important for the Dutch flower auctions at which more than twenty million flowers are sold on a typical day.

You might have also heard that Dutch auctions have been used to sell shares of companies. For example, when Google went public in the summer of 2004, it was reported to have sold its shares using the Dutch auction. An important distinction exists, however, between a particular lot of flowers in Aalsmeer and the shares of an Internet company: the lot of flowers is unique, having idiosyncratic features, whereas one share of Google stock is the same as any other share of Google stock. This difference suggests that auctions can be used to sell just one object or many of them, a feature we will explore later. It also allows us to note that the mechanism used to sell shares of Google stock at its initial public offering is, as we will later see, not what economists classify as a Dutch auction.

Dutch and English auctions are dynamic in the sense that price changes are visible to bidders as the auction progresses, hence the term "open." This is especially true at the English auction with paddles being raised. In short, at either auction, bidders observe how the price evolves. Today, however, many auctions are held electronically, with bidders accessing a computer server on which the auction is conducted virtually. For example, the Portland Fish Exchange (PFEX) in Maine, the oldest all-display, fresh seafood auction in the United States, is an electronic auction. At the PFEX, some potential buyers arrive at the auction house to inspect the day's fish in person; these potential bidders often sit at computers in a common room, each vying to secure fresh fish to process later that day. Often wholesalers hire professional graders to identify lots that might be of interest to them. These grades are then passed to offsite bidders, who access the auction market via remote terminals. Nevertheless, the information revealed to bidders concerning how prices change is the same: at English auctions, bidders know the current high bid, whereas at Dutch auctions, bidders are aware of the current asking price. Consequently we include in our definition of the open format those mechanisms that are implemented on computers, provided that the dynamic features concerning the asking price are present and information concerning the current price is made known to all participants.

In mentioning the PFEX, we also highlight the fact that the taxonomy described in table 1 is not comprehensive. For instance, the PFEX is actually a hybrid Dutch–English auction: the price starts at a set opening price determined by the auctioneer and initially drops; when one bidder expresses interest in a certain type (size and species) of fish, the price then rises in one-cent increments until no one is willing to increase the price further.

The other commonly studied auction format is the sealed bid. At sealed-bid auctions, buyers indicate how much they are willing to pay for the object on sale by submitting a bid in secret to the auctioneer, traditionally in a sealed envelope, hence the name. Each bidder can only submit one bid, and thus tenders that bid knowing nothing about the bids submitted by rivals. Once all the bids have been submitted by an announced time, the auctioneer evaluates them and awards the object to the bidder who has tendered the highest bid.

Although the winner at sealed-bid auctions is the highest bidder, as described in table 1, at least two different pricing rules can be used to determine the transaction price paid by the winner. At *first-price, sealed-bid auctions*, the winning bidder pays the highest bid tendered. Since the winning bidder is the one committing to pay the most for the item at auction, this format is also referred to as a *pay-your-bid auction*. In contrast, at a *second-price, sealed-bid auction*, the winning bidder pays the second-highest bid tendered. This small difference in the pricing rules generates important differences in behavior that will be made clear in chapter 3. To develop some intuition for this, consider the difference in the pricing rule: under pay-your-bid pricing, a bidder's own offer determines the payment required, while under the second-price rule, it is the offer made by a rival bidder that determines the payment of the winner.

Even though many people do not realize it, first-price, sealed-bid auctions are employed extensively and play central roles in the decisions made by policy makers in most countries. Laws in most democratic countries require that governments make purchasing decisions using a process referred to as *procurement*. For example, in 1974, in accordance with the Office of Federal Procurement Policy Act, the US Congress established the Office of Federal Procurement Policy and charged this office with the responsibility of designing procurement policies, procedures, provisions, and regulations. In short, if a government agency seeks to purchase a good or service, then it often must solicit bids from several suppliers, sometimes just a few of them. Interested firms submit bids that are reviewed by the government agency on a set date at a specific time. Typically the contract is awarded to the firm willing to provide the good or service at the lowest price. Thus the public procurement process is exactly like a first-price, sealed-bid auction, except that the winning bidder is *paid* to provide a good or service and the winner is determined by the firm asking to be paid the least. Consequently these procurement auctions are often referred to as *low-price, sealed-bid* auctions or *reverse* auctions.

In short, auctions are not just used to sell objects but also to purchase them (or services) from a set of potential suppliers. Public procurement is a critical component of government spending; the US government spends hundreds of billions of dollars on procurement each year. In fact the White House reports that more than one of every six dollars spent by the federal government is paid to such contractors. Ensuring the government can complete tasks in the cheapest way is such an important objective that we dedicate an entire chapter to procurement.

The second-price, sealed-bid auction is commonly referred to as the *Vickrey* auction, in honor of the Nobel laureate William S. Vickrey who first analyzed this type of auction in the early 1960s, even though stamp collectors had used second-price, sealed-bid auctions during the late nineteenth century, and perhaps before. Consider a philatelist living in a remote location during the 1800s and seeking to sell some stamps. An English auction held locally would likely not have attracted a large group of interested bidders. Even if some interested collectors were to attend the auction, the competition would likely not have been great, thus potentially depressing prices. In contrast, if stamp sales could be publicized and bids submitted through the mail, then the seller could attract greater interest from collectors who might have been unable to travel, thus generating higher prices for the seller.

Although the Vickrey auction also has many attractive theoretical properties, it is rarely used in practice. Much of the Vickrey auction's practical value will be noted later when we illustrate how this type of auction can be extended to accommodate multiple units of the same good or even several different objects.

Even though we focus on first- and second-price sealed-bid auctions in this book, nothing prevents an auctioneer from using other pricing rules. For example, when awarding a procurement contract using an auction, some government agencies choose the bidder whose tender is closest to the average bid. In Italy, between 2000 and 2006, procurement contracts were awarded using an average-bid pricing rule whenever five or more bidders submitted tenders. How did it work?

Bidders were provided a benchmark cost derived by engineers that the government felt was reasonable to complete some task. They then submitted sealed bids representing discounts relative to this benchmark, for example, one hundred thousand euros below the benchmark. The award process worked as follows: the highest and lowest 10 percent of bids were discarded immediately. An average was then computed based on the remaining bids. A second average was then computed using the bids that did not get originally discarded, but using only the bids that exceeded the first average computed. The bidder whose tender was closest to, but lower than, this second average was declared the winner. Although this may sound like the bidders were essentially playing a guessing game for the right to perform a task for the government, and that the government might have done just as well by randomly assigning the contract, we suggest later why this might have been an attractive way of determining the winning tender.

When to Use Auctions, and Why

Auctions are constantly being used in new environments where well-established markets do not exist, and little is known about the true value of an object. Even though the rules may become increasingly complex, in more sophisticated settings where uncertainty is great, auctions perform a critical service referred to as *price discovery*. The structure imposed by the auction format and the pricing rule ensures that prices are formed transparently. Price discovery allows for fair and voluntary trades to take place.

Simply put, auctions are a way of equating demand and supply. An example may make this clear. Suppose that you have a ticket to see a local baseball game on a given evening, but when game day arrives, you realize that

Simply put, auctions are a way of equating demand and supply.

responsibilities at work will prevent you from attending the sold-out game. Not wanting the ticket to be wasted, you check to see whether any of your friends might be interested: four express interest in the ticket. One way to decide who should get the ticket is to draw lots, that is, to hold a raffle. Although this may seem fair, it does not guarantee that the friend who values the ticket the most will win the ticket. Because of this, economists would refer to the raffle as an *inefficient* allocation mechanism. You decide instead that the efficient way to allocate the ticket is to sell it at auction. Is the auction an efficient selling mechanism? Let's see.

Suppose that one friend values the ticket at $10, another at $7, a third would pay up to $5, and the last values the ticket at $1. In figure 1 we plot these values in descending order. The lines below the respective price points indicate how many tickets you would need to have if you were to approach each of your friends with a take-it-or-leave-it offer. For example, at $4, you would get three "Yes!" responses (from the friends willing to pay $10, $7, and $5). As the asking price increases, fewer friends are interested in your offer. Economics students will recognize the staircase pattern as representing your friends' demand for the baseball ticket. Since you do not have three tickets to give to each of your friends, a request for $4 will not suffice, so you must raise the asking price until only one friend is willing to pay for the ticket you have for sale.

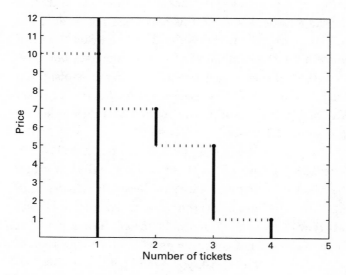

Figure 1   Demand and supply for baseball ticket

Figure 1 also depicts the supply of tickets—the vertical line at the quantity one. This line reflects that you are willing to sell the ticket for any amount of money, but that you have just one ticket to sell. The mantra "supply equals demand" determines who should get the ticket and what the traded price will be. It is clear that the ticket should go to the friend willing to pay the most to attend the game. How much should that friend pay for the ticket? Well, at any price below $7, two friends will demand tickets, and at any price above $10, no friends will demand tickets. Therefore a region of possible prices exists between $7 and $10. What price should be charged?

Now imagine conducting an English auction among your four friends. For low asking prices, competition will ensue allowing the price to rise. As the price ascends to $7, consider the standing bidder is the friend willing to pay $10. None of your other friends will respond to higher asking prices, meaning the friend willing to pay $10 should get the ticket and pay $7 for it. The value $7 represents a sacred concept in economics referred to as *opportunity cost*. Economists are a bit pessimistic, feeling that nothing in the world is without some cost. The opportunity cost to you personally of a day off from work might be the wages you could have otherwise earned. Likewise choosing to see a movie on a Friday night might mean that you gave up the opportunity to take in a play. Opportunity costs can also be considered from a resource-allocation perspective, in which costs are borne (benefits are forgone) by society. A number of important Picasso paintings are privately owned. The opportunity cost might reflect the benefit other private collectors would gain from hanging the paintings on their own walls or, perhaps, the aggregate benefit to society from showcasing them in museums. In this sense, opportunity cost represents the value of a resource in its next-best alternative. In the case of your ticket to the local baseball game, the second-highest valuation for the ticket represents the benefit forgone when your friend with the highest valuation has the opportunity to attend the game.

Let's take stock here; a lot has been accomplished. The hypothetical auction you've just conducted achieved the transfer of the ticket that has several attractive properties. First, a reasonable price was discovered and the allocation problem solved. Second, the ticket was awarded to the friend who was willing to pay the most to see the game; such an allocation is referred to as *efficient* because the object went to the bidder who valued the ticket the most. Third, the price discovered through the auction represents the opportunity cost of the ticket, the value of the ticket in its next-best use. Fourth, the auction generated attractive outcomes for both the buyer and the seller—in this example, you earned $7 and kept your friends happy, and the winning friend got to see a game at a price that is less than $10: two people are made better off, and no one is made worse off. Economists refer to this as a *Pareto improvement*.

Missing from the example above is the element of time. Not only do auctions have the attractive allocational properties discussed but the rules can be structured so that such allocations are achieved in a timely manner. You need not look beyond your own childhood to realize this. It's likely that you and your friends or siblings left abandoned games of Monopoly for hours, perhaps days, before an adult "suggested" the game be picked up and put away. Frequently the games were likely drawn out because you just could not land on the property needed to complete ownership of a color group. The original Parker Brothers rules actually dictate that the all-responsible Banker also serve as an Auctioneer. If you land on a property that no one owns, then you have the right to buy the property at the printed price. Often overlooked, however, is the sentence that soon follows: "If you do not wish to buy the property, the Banker sells it at auction to the highest bidder." It seems the Parker Brothers understood that auctions are a way of allocating goods quickly. (If only they had specified the type of auction that should be used!) Unfortunately, many of us did not read the rules fully and were left shamefully explaining to our friends why a game remained unfinished.

Thus far our primary goal has been to provide you with an appreciation of auctions and the role they play in society. Central to the study of auctions, and implicit in the baseball ticket story above, is the notion of asymmetric information: the seller of an object does not know any bidder's valuation for that object. Were information complete, the seller could just approach the bidder having the highest valuation and make a take-it-or-leave-it offer at, or perhaps slightly below, that bidder's valuation. The seller might threaten to refuse sale under any other terms if the offer is rejected; the buyer might be intransigent. This is referred to as the *holdout* problem; a transaction cost is introduced because of the holdout problem—delay. One by-product of an auction is that this transaction cost is ameliorated.

Alas, the seller probably does not know any given bidder's valuation. Moreover the seller likely does not even know which bidder values the object the most, so negotiating with the bidder valuing the object most is probably impossible, especially in our increasingly global economy. Informational asymmetries indicate a need for a rich way of aggregating information before transactions are made. Auctions make explicit that aggregation process. Additionally, in our example, the auction served as a public, transparent way of allocating the ticket. None of your friends will be offended because each agreed to respect the rules and outcome of the auction.

Although unimportant in the baseball ticket example, one objective the seller may have is to garner the most for the object sold—earn the most revenue. Asymmetric information constrains the seller from extracting all of the value from the buyers. Consequently the seller fosters competition among interested buyers to drive up revenues. An auction is an efficient way to generate competition, even when the number of buyers is relatively small, say, just two or three. Because the seller is constrained from getting the highest valuation bidder to reveal completely their value of the object, the seller generates competition among the other bidders to drive up the price as high as possible. This could take the form of constructing rules within an auction to generate aggressive bidding among a set of buyers or it could mean casting as wide a net as possible when attracting potentially interested buyers to the auction. Despite these efforts, because the seller does not know how much any one of the bidders values the object, it is difficult for the seller to earn a price exactly equal to the object's value to the winner. Consequently the winner of an auction earns a surplus as well.

Asymmetric information exists among buyers, too. Those interested in purchasing the object probably know very little about the object's worth to other auction participants—either the seller or rival bidders. When uncertainty concerning the object's true value exists and where it is important to allocate the object in the most efficient way, the auction is your BFF.

With the collapse of the Soviet Union, how did the former republics transition from planned economies to market-based economies? In part, by privatizing state-owned assets, which were often sold at auction. Auctions are ideal for selling objects that have no standard value. Sometimes, the object at auction may be unique, as in the case of formerly state-owned enterprises; other times, auctions are used to sell several objects whose prices are likely to vary depending on daily circumstances. For example, the world's largest fish market in the Tsukiji district of Tokyo uses the auction. With fish, uncertainty exists concerning both demand and supply; predicting market-clearing prices is difficult. On the one hand, fishing vessels cannot promise certain catches because fish move constantly in the ocean; weather patterns are unpredictable too. On the other hand, the demands of restaurants and retailers as well as food processors fluctuate from period to period. For example, even today many Roman Catholics still eat fish on Fridays. In addition the quality of the fish can vary depending on how the fish are caught, how long they have been on ice, the size of the fish, and so forth. Fish are also one of the most perishable of commodities. High search costs mean that auctions are an effective way to distribute fish.

On the National Public Radio program *All Things Considered*, a land auction in Iowa captured the attention of the show's producer when bidders were observed checking their phones for current corn-price quotations. Why? Prices of farmland in Iowa, in part, derive from the price of corn. Ethanol, which can be produced from corn, can serve as an additive to gasoline. Thus prices of Iowa farmland are influenced by events at the Chicago Board of Trade and on Wall Street as well as overseas in oil-producing countries.

Even though all this may sound complicated, studying auctions is relatively straightforward because the economic environments are very structured: by design, the rules are stated explicitly and are often quite easy to understand. Hence these rules can be mapped cleanly into models of how bidders will behave, which then allow you to focus on deeper issues, such as the expected revenues earned by the seller and the efficiency of an object's allocation. Indeed, over the past sixty years, economists have made remarkable progress in studying auctions—both theoretically and empirically. Auctions are one area of economics where theoretical and empirical work is most closely linked, in large part because researchers have constructed ways of marrying real-world data with the theoretical models. With that said, let's start constructing some models of auctions!

MODELING AUCTIONS

In this book we use economic theory as the lens through which to view auctions. Economic theorists focus on decision-making. Decision makers are constrained: scarcity exists everywhere. For example, people have finite amounts of time and money. Such constraints limit what people can achieve. In writing down models that describe human behavior, economic actors are assumed to optimize. Perhaps consumers try to maximize their satisfaction from purchases. Firms might attempt to produce something in the most cost-effective way possible. A government could be interested in achieving the best outcome for the poorest members of society. Purposeful pursuit of these objectives guides decision making. Economists often focus on equilibrium outcomes. Equilibrium is a situation where, holding constant all other relevant factors that influence decisions, no decision maker has an incentive to change behavior.

Equilibrium is a situation where, holding constant all other relevant factors that influence decisions, no decision maker has an incentive to change behavior.

Although the triumvirate of hypotheses—scarcity, optimization, and equilibrium—is essential to nearly all economic models, we refine our perspective even further. Specifically, we note that many choices are made in strategic settings where interdependencies exist among decision makers, particularly among the payoffs those decision makers receive. Bidders who do not understand how to internalize the behavior of others are at a disadvantage. Unfortunately, such interdependencies are often overlooked.

In 1971 Martin Shubik proposed the following auction experiment, which you can try among friends. Consider an oral, ascending-price auction where the highest bidder wins the object for sale. Instead of having just the winner pay the seller, require that the second-highest bidder pay the seller too. (Later, when we investigate all-pay auctions, you will see that it is not uncommon to require payment from losing bidders as well.) With these rules understood by a group of already skeptical friends, inform them that the object being sold is a $10 bill.

Now that they are all smiling, propose a starting bid of 25 cents. Someone will surely accept an opening price of a quarter for a sawbuck. Raise the bid to 50 cents. Predictably, another friend will participate. At this point you as the seller should be delighted. To be sure, only 75 cents has been committed, and you must eventually make $10, but think about how the bidders should respond given their situations. At first, they will jokingly continue to raise the price, but at some point someone will realize what is happening. Suppose that two friends (often others will join in the "fun") keep raising the price. Imagine one friend is leading the auction at $4, while another has committed to $3. In order to win the item, the friend who owes you $3 has an incentive to raise the price because the new leader will then owe you some amount less than $10, but will receive $10 at the close of the auction. In short, a profit remains possible which, however small, is better than owing you $3. Once the bidder who has committed $4 has been overtaken, the incentive to outbid the leader remains. When both bidders have committed to more than $5 each, you are golden. A critical threshold has been met: you are in the money. From your friends' perspective, this is irrelevant as each individually still has the opportunity to come out of the auction having earned a profit. Moreover each still has incentive to outbid the other, so they will continue to increase bids. At $10, however, reality will surely set in: both the leader and the follower are going to lose money. The sad thing is that they will also recognize something else—the need to continue bidding. Regardless of the highest price at auction, the second-highest bidder prefers to outbid the leading bidder in order to minimize losses.

This experiment has never failed to make us money. The pricing rule exploits the failure of many people to internalize the decisions of others—to think strategically.

As Shubik noted in his original article, it works even better if your friends have already had something to drink.

Understanding the interdependencies among bidders and how the rules of the auction affect bidder incentives is critical to understanding how bidders behave as well as expected outcomes. Often only small numbers of bidders participate at auctions. Game theory is a critical tool when analyzing behavior in such situations—specifically, how to internalize the decisions of rival bidders. In this vein, we describe how auctions are modeled by economists and how bidders are predicted to behave in such settings. Understanding bidder behavior is central to appreciating some attractive properties of auctions.

Before diving into the material, we should note that modeling auctions is often mathematically technical. We will not wade through this technical minutiae but rather illustrate in nontechnical ways how economists study auctions. In so doing, we hope not only to justify the approach taken by economists but also to equip you to understand the issues at work.

Auctions as Games

Game theory is a collection of techniques that permits the analysis of strategic situations when interdependencies among decision makers exist—situations where the payoffs are not determined by just one decision maker's action but rather by the collective choices of all decision makers involved. At an auction, whether you are awarded the object for sale depends on how your bid relates to those of your rivals.

Consider one of best-known examples in game theory—the Prisoners' Dilemma. In this game, two suspects of a crime, Alice and Bob, have been arrested and are kept in separate cells, each being interrogated by authorities. Suppose that the penalties each suspect will incur depend not only on her or his action but also the action of the other suspect. In table 2 we depict the payoffs to two strategies—confess or silent. The pairs of numbers in each of the four cells represent the number of years of jail time that each will receive based on the outcome that the interrogator obtains; the negative numbers indicate years of time lost. In our notation, the number that precedes the comma represents Alice's payoff, while the number after the comma is the payoff Bob receives. In analyzing this game, we assume that suspects prefer less jail time to more. The payoffs summarize each player's preferences; considering other objectives would simply mean changing the values we have assigned each player. Regardless, the payoffs, which depend on the choices of both players, determine how Alice and Bob rank the outcomes.

Suppose that the game is played just once, so reputation is unimportant. Before considering strategy, let's walk

Table 2 Payoffs in Prisoners' Dilemma game

- -

		Bob	
		Confess	Silent
Alice	Confess	−10, −10	0, −15
	Silent	−15, 0	−1, −1

through some interpretations of what the payoff matrix tells us. First, if both Alice and Bob confess to the crime, they each earn ten years in prison. Second, if both Alice and Bob remain silent, the authorities will have a tough time establishing guilt in court and can only ensure that the suspects each get one year in jail. Finally, if only one suspect confesses, which involves revealing that both were responsible for the crime, but the other remains silent, then the confessor gets off free because of amnesty and the suspect who remained silent gets the harshest possible penalty—fifteen years, perhaps because of the irrefutable case prosecutors have built using the other partner's confession. This characterization of the setting is not unrealistic. As an example, under the Corporate Leniency Policy a cartel-member firm reporting illegal actions of the group is granted immunity under certain conditions.

Given this payoff matrix, what do you predict will happen? To begin, we need to understand the information structure of the game—that is, who knows what when decisions are made. For now, assume that everything you as the reader have seen written here is also known by the players themselves: Alice and Bob can model this game in the same way we have. Each has the choice to confess or to remain silent and each knows the other's preferences over the possible outcomes. Game theorists refer to this as *complete information*. Assume further that each player knows the other player knows the rules, players, strategies, and payoffs, and that each player knows the other player knows her/his rival knows the information contained in the matrix above, and that Alice and Bob both know that the other knows the other player knows her/his rival knows this information, and so forth *ad infinitum*. Game theorists refer to this latter assumption as *common knowledge*.

By looking at the payoffs, you can see that the best joint outcome involves both remaining silent—only two total years are served, one year each for Alice and Bob. This seems like an attractive prediction to make in this setting. With that in mind, let's think a bit deeper about each suspect's preferences and incentives within this environment. Specifically, what would Bob do if he believed Alice was going to confess? Well, if he too confessed, he would receive ten years in prison; in contrast, if he remained silent he would receive fifteen years in prison. Therefore, if Bob thinks Alice will confess, he too will want to confess because he will then get five fewer years' jail time. Thus Bob's *best response* to Alice's strategy of confess is also to confess.

Now, what will Bob do if he believes Alice will remain silent? Well, if Bob confesses he will be pardoned and spend no time in jail, whereas if he too keeps mum he will spend a year in jail. Alice might be a vindictive person, so Bob may fear consequences when tattling, but he will also have fifteen years to take up a new life if he confesses, given he thinks she will be silent. Therefore, assuming that Bob prefers no jail time to one year in jail, his best response to Alice's strategy of keeping silent is to confess. In this game, regardless of the strategy Alice chooses, Bob does the best for himself by confessing. For Bob, confessing is referred to as a *strictly dominant strategy*.

Because this game is symmetric (Alice's payoffs mirror Bob's), you can see that our discussion above holds if we reverse the roles of Alice and Bob, and walk through the hypothetical situations concerning what Alice might do for each action Bob might take. Therefore both players will confess, certainly not the jointly optimal outcome. Therein lies the paradox, and also why the game is referred to as the *Prisoners' Dilemma*.

This problem is simple for game theorists to solve because a rational player will always play the strictly dominant strategy. The notion of a dominant strategy allows you to make predictions for some of the auctions already described. Unfortunately, dominance will only get us so far in our investigation of auctions. So, before proceeding, we should note that dominant strategies need not always exist. The game above can be perturbed in simple ways so that dominance breaks down. For example, suppose that whenever he confesses, Bob incurs psychological damage that is the equivalent of three years' jail time (in addition to any time he actually serves), and Alice knows this; we continue to focus on games of complete information. A modified version of this game has the payoff matrix presented in table 3.

To find the equilibrium of this new game, note that Alice's incentives remain unchanged; she still has a strictly dominant strategy to confess. However, Bob no longer has a dominant strategy: if Alice confesses, then Bob's best response is to confess as the equivalent of thirteen years in prison (ten in actual prison and three years' worth of psychological damage) still outranks fifteen years behind bars; if Alice remains silent, then Bob's best response is to remain silent because one year of jail is better than three years of psychological damage. Bob no longer has a dominant strategy; his optimal behavior now depends on the strategy he believes Alice will employ.

Table 3 Modified payoff matrix

- -

| | | Bob | |
		Confess	Silent
Alice	Confess	–10, –13	0, –15
	Silent	–15, –3	–1, –1

A *Nash equilibrium* is a collection of strategies for which no player wants to change her or his strategy, given her or his beliefs about the strategy chosen by the other players.

Although this game is still dominance solvable, we have modified it in order to introduce a notion of equilibrium that will be important later. John F. Nash shared the Nobel Prize in Economics "for [his] pioneering analysis of equilibria in the theory of noncooperative games." Nash became a household name in 2001 when *A Beautiful Mind*, the biographical film about his life, won four Academy Awards, including Best Picture. Nash made a number of extremely important contributions to the analysis of games, but here we will focus only on his notion of equilibrium. A *Nash equilibrium* is a collection of strategies (in the example above, a pair of strategies) for which no player wants to change her or his strategy, given her or his beliefs about the strategy chosen by the other players. (In a Nash equilibrium, players' beliefs are accurate, so beliefs and behavior are consonant.) Note the prediction in this modified game remains the same—both players confess, but it is not because both Alice and Bob rationally play their dominant strategies. Instead, appealing to Nash's equilibrium concept: given Alice is confessing, it is in Bob's interest to confess; given Bob is confessing, it is in Alice's interest to confess. That is, having players confess is a stable outcome in the sense that no player will want to change her or his strategy given the rival also confesses.

With this basic understanding of strategies and equilibria in games, let's return to the world of auctions. Every model of a game has four main elements: the players; the

Every model of a game has four main elements: the players; the strategies available to the players; the players' preferences over all possible outcomes, which we represent by payoffs; and the information structure.

strategies available to the players; the players' preferences over all possible outcomes, which we represent by payoffs; and the information structure. In auction games the players are the seller and the bidders; the strategies are the bids. It seems reasonable to assume that when bidders are unsuccessful in winning the object at auction, they earn nothing, whereas when a bidder wins an auction, the payoff is the difference between what that bidder was willing to pay for an object and what was actually paid for the object. At this point you might have realized something important: the players in auction games *do not know* the value of the object (and therefore the payoffs) to rivals. In fact it was exactly this point—asymmetric information—that formed the basis for our earlier discussion concerning the environments in which auctions are most helpful. Using the vocabulary of game theory, auctions are referred to as games of *incomplete information*. Were Alice and Bob rivals at an auction, it would be inappropriate to assume that one bidder knew how much the object for sale is worth to the other.

The change in the information structure is important. Because of this change, we must refine our notion of a Nash equilibrium slightly. John Harsanyi shared the Nobel Prize with John F. Nash (and Reinhard Selten) for developing ways to analyze games of incomplete information. Bidders vying for an object at auction have valuations that are unknown to the other players. Firms competing to win a contract for the right to perform a service or to provide a good for the government have costs that are unknown by rival firms. The unknown valuations or costs (more generally referred to by game theorists as the *types* of the players) mean the payoffs of rivals are the private information of those players. Consequently bidders compete in an environment where they are unsure of the payoffs of outcomes to rivals. Referring back to our Prisoners' Dilemma example, suppose that Alice is unsure whether Bob is solely self-interested or is someone who would be guilt-ridden were he to confess. Although Bob knows what type of person he is, Alice does not: an asymmetry of information exists. To model how the players should behave, we need to specify how likely Bob is to be the selfish versus the remorseful type. Harsanyi recognized this need and resolved it by introducing a new (albeit nonstrategic) player, commonly referred to as *Nature*. Nature randomly assigns a type to each player according to specific probabilities. This type is known to the player, but rivals only know the likelihood of each type's arising.

Modifying the components of a strategic game with complete information, a strategic game of incomplete information involves the following elements: the players; for each player, a set of possible types; a fixed probability distribution describing the likelihood that every possible combination of types (one for each player) is realized; for each player, a set of strategies available to the players; pay-offs that each player earns for all possible combinations of strategies. The fundamental difference is that now each player can be of a different type—the player's private information. The other players have some understanding of what type each rival might be. This information is described by an urn of types that is assumed common knowledge. Bob's urn contains different fractions of selfish and remorseful balls that Nature draws for him.

Implicit in the last feature of payoffs is an understanding of what strategies are available to the players. The concept of a strategy in a game of incomplete information is a bit more complicated. Specifically, for a given player, a strategy prescribes a feasible action that the player should adopt for each and every possible type the player might be. One way to think of a strategy is a complete plan that prescribes which action should be played for each type. Revisiting Alice and Bob when Bob may be selfish or may be remorseful, Alice's payoffs are the same regardless of Bob's type. Alice has only one type; for her, a strategy is simply a possible action—confess or silent. Bob has two possible types; for him, a strategy is one action given he is the selfish type *and* another given he is the remorseful type.

To put this in terms of an auction, suppose that you want to bid for an object but do not know its quality beforehand because you cannot attend the auction to inspect the object; quality, however, determines your valuation.

Suppose that you have a friend who is willing to attend the auction for you and can determine the true quality of the object. Thus your friend will be able to determine how much the object is worth to you—your valuation. What your friend possesses in quality detection, however, he lacks in business acumen: you need to tell him what to bid, but you cannot contact the friend between the time quality is learned and when the bidding takes place. Therefore you must provide the friend with a rule that says exactly what bid should be tendered for each and every possible quality (valuation) that exists. Although this is a quirky story, especially in a world connected by smartphones, we hope it illustrates that in auction games you want to find a rule that takes each valuation and returns a bid for all possible valuations a bidder might have. If you can specify such a rule, then your friend will know how to bid for you at the auction—translate quality into valuation, reference the rule, and then bid that amount on your behalf. Mathematicians refer to strategies that map types into actions as *functions*.

Again, an equilibrium is a collection of strategies, but for games in which players have private information, the concept of a Nash equilibrium receives a qualifier and is referred to as a *Bayes–Nash equilibrium*. Reverend Thomas Bayes made important contributions to the field of probability in the eighteenth century—specifically, Bayes' theorem, a theorem that can be used to update players' beliefs.

For example, in dynamic games actions taken early in the game can influence players' beliefs about rivals' unknown types later in the game. In fact, because probabilities play a central role in games of incomplete information, such games are also referred to as *Bayesian games*. Having been exposed to some essential concepts that you will need from game theory, we now explore some specific assumptions that we initially maintain but then relax in later parts of the book.

Baseline Model

Levering what you have learned of game theory, let's apply it to an auction game. The players are the seller and the bidders. The strategies are the bids. The bidders have types that are private information; the types are the bidders' valuations. The payoffs are the valuations minus the traded price. Don't forget, however, that valuations are randomly determined by Nature. We model valuations as random variables, which means that bidders view their rivals' valuations as unknown draws from some urn.

To understand this last statement better, let's introduce a story that illustrates the moving parts. Imagine bidders have valuations that are positive, whole numbers that range from one to one hundred, with each possible number having an equal chance of occurring. Thus the probability a bidder has the valuation 22 is the same as the probability that the bidder has the valuation 83 or the valuation 47—one in a hundred or 1 percent. One physical model of this process would involve putting one hundred ping-pong balls into a big urn, where the numbers 1, 2, 3, ..., 99, 100, have been inscribed on the sequence of balls. Having placed the balls in the urn, shake them thoroughly—to mix them well. Bring all the bidders at the auction into the room and describe to them the process just completed so that each is aware of the possible values as well as the chances of drawing each value. Ask one of the bidders to select a ball, remember the ball's number but tell no one that number; inform the bidder that the drawn number is her valuation of the object at auction. Have the bidder then place the selected ball back into the urn, which you again shake well. Ask another bidder to come forward and to select a ball, repeating the process until all bidders have received valuations.

This description involves a very specific kind of random variable, one with a discrete number of possible outcomes, each having the same chance as the others. That all bidders know each possible valuation as well as how likely a bidder is to receive each possible valuation are very important assumptions. In the baseline model such information is common knowledge. This is what we mean when we say that the urn describing how types are generated is commonly understood. Because each bidder is the only one to observe the ball drawn, this reflects the type (valuation), which is the private information that the bidder realizes for the object at auction.

This story also allows us to outline some basic assumptions that are maintained in our initial investigation of auctions. Specifically, valuations are random variables that are independently and identically distributed. Independence means that when one bidder draws a valuation it in no way alters the chances of rival bidders obtaining certain valuations. Two random variables are independent if the realization of one does not affect the probability over the potential outcomes of the other. In our setting, when you draw your valuation for the object at auction, it tells you nothing about what your rivals' valuations will be. Valuations are identically distributed because each bidder draws a ball from the same urn.

One shortcoming of our example is that bidders are prevented from having valuations that are not round numbers. For example, someone might value a bottle of Caymus Vineyards 2012 Cabernet Sauvignon at $58.83. Admitting infinitely many valuations actually makes life easier for auction researchers. In all of the results presented below, we assume infinitely many different valuations. Thus, rather than consider discrete probability functions, like our urn of balls, we consider continuous random variables, the ability to choose any number on a portion of the number line. In figure 2 we present three examples of probability density functions, which are relations that convey the relative likelihood that a random variable takes on certain values. The flat horizontal line represents a uniform probability distribution, which is the continuous version of the urn of balls described earlier. It means that drawing a valuation between $10 and $15 is just as likely as drawing a valuation between $32 and $37, $89.25 and $94.25, or any other pair of numbers $5 apart. The normal distribution is the bell-shaped curve peaking in the middle of the figure. In this case valuations are more likely to occur in, say, the $40 to $60 range than in any other $20 range. The exponential distribution, in contrast, puts most of the weight on low valuations; high valuations are much less likely to occur. Differences in the urns from which valuations are drawn can imply differences in the behavior that bidders exhibit at auction.

Within this model, a bidder does not care *who* the other competing bidders are before the balls are drawn from the urn as nothing distinguishes one bidder from another. In the Prisoners' Dilemma examples, this would be like saying that Alice doesn't need to know whether she is detained with Bob or Charles, just so long that she knows she is being questioned alongside one of them. At an auction within this environment then, bidders need only know *how many* rival bidders are vying for the object at auction.

Thus far we have been vague concerning what is sold at auction and how the participants at the auction feel about

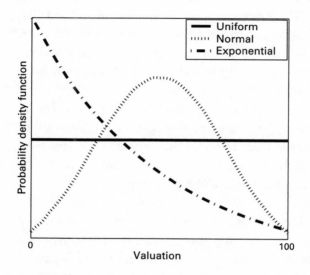

Figure 2 Some probability density functions

the object. To highlight important differences, contrast buying a copy of your high school yearbook with buying a jar of coins at auction. The value of the yearbook is likely driven by the intrinsic value you personally place on the yearbook. Before bidding, you will need to think about the sentimental value of owning the yearbook. If you were told the value someone else put on that yearbook, would it change the object's worth to you? Probably not. Knowing someone else's value can provide you with a strategic advantage in how to bid at the auction, but the intrinsic worth of the object to you is probably unchanged by this revelation. Auction researchers refer to economic environments like this as the *independent private-values (IPV) paradigm*. The word "independent" comes from our discussion of independence above in which (private) valuations are modeled as random variables whose realizations represent draws from an urn and are in no way correlated with other players' valuations.

At the other extreme, consider the value of a jar of coins—pennies, nickels, dimes, and quarters of different numbers all mixed together—where you are prohibited from counting the individual coins until after the auction has ended. In this case neither you nor any other bidder knows with certainty the actual monetary value of the coins in the jar. Each bidder likely has a different estimate of the amount of money; those differences lead to different bids. Although the value of the jar is unknown before the auction, after the auction, when the coins have been counted, the value is common to all. Here, knowing someone else's estimate of the amount of money in the jar can be informative—not just in a strategic sense as in the case of the high school yearbook, but also in refining your own estimate of the value of the coins. (You would then have two estimates to use when predicting the jar's value.) Auction researchers refer to this as the *pure common-value paradigm*.

Note that the driving force behind variation in the observed bids differs between the private-values and the common-value paradigms: in the former case, bidders value the object at auction differently, while in the latter the object has the same value to all bidders—even though this value is unknown at the time of auction and bidders have different estimates of this value.

In our initial discussion and in the benchmark model, we assume the IPV paradigm. Recall that when we described valuations as random variables within the context of a model, there we considered not only independently distributed but also identically distributed random variables. Auction researchers refer to this as the *symmetric* IPV paradigm. Before the valuations have been drawn, all bidders are effectively the same—symmetric. Later we demonstrate that relaxing the assumption that the valuation of each bidder is drawn from the same urn alters important properties of auction outcomes. To be clear, however, when assuming a common urn, we are not saying that all bidders have the same valuation, just that their valuations represent realizations of random variables drawn from the same urn (for example, the uniform, normal, or exponential distributions shown in figure 2). We use the IPV setting as a starting point for understanding some deeper issues and complicating factors that arise when studying auctions.

Finally, before considering bidder behavior at auctions, we need to discuss the attitudes of bidders toward risk because they will be making decisions in environments that involve uncertainty. Initially, we assume that bidders are risk neutral. What does that mean? Consider the following thought experiment involving a coin toss: if a head occurs, then you earn $100; if it's a tail, then you earn $0. Suppose this coin-flipping experiment is conducted many times; assume that the probability of either a head or a tail is the same—a fair coin: half the time heads, half the time tails. On average, half the time $100 will be paid and half the time $0 will be paid; the average payment is $50. A risk-neutral person is indifferent between playing this coin-flipping game and receiving $50 with certainty. In contrast, a risk-averse person would prefer a sure payment of less than $50 to the coin-flipping opportunity. A risk-lover would require more than $50 to give up the opportunity to play the coin-flipping game. In our baseline model we will assume that bidders are risk neutral.

In this chapter we have touched on a number of different, important topics. Understandably, you may be surprised by the amount of structure required to model bidding at auctions. All of this structure is necessary. For at auctions, incomplete information reigns: each bidder has some private information concerning his valuation but typically knows little about the valuations of rivals. Bidders know how many rivals they face, feasible valuations each rival might have, and how likely such valuations are to be realized. This information is commonly understood by all bidders.

We began the chapter by noting that most economic models rest on three hypotheses: scarcity, optimization, and equilibrium. At auctions scarcity is manifest by there being just one object. The outcome of an auction is determined by the behavior of all the players at the auction, each holding private information. Given this, payoffs involve probabilities—when you bid at auction, there is some probability that you will win and then earn a positive payoff, and some probability that you will lose and earn nothing. Risk-neutral bidders seek to maximize expected payoffs; that is their objective. Valuations are likely determined by a combination of bidders' personal feelings for the object at auction, their budgets, and so forth. These factors dictate a bidder's maximum willingness to pay. Finally, we focus on the Bayes–Nash equilibrium as the equilibrium concept. This means each player chooses a strategy that maximizes expected payoffs given their beliefs about rivals' types and the strategies chosen by rival bidders. In the next chapter we use these tools to investigate bidder behavior.

BIDDER BEHAVIOR

Recall the coin-flipping experiment of the previous chapter and imagine you are asked to participate in such an experiment: a coin is flipped; if heads, you win $100; if tails, you earn nothing. When the coin is flipped repeatedly and you are compensated by the appropriate amount with each toss, on average, you will earn $50 per coin toss. We refer to $50, the average amount won per toss, as the *expected payoff* of one toss in the coin-flipping experiment.

This example shares some common features with the types of auctions we discussed in chapter 1. At all of those auctions, you earn something (win the object) when you are the highest bidder, but you earn nothing otherwise. The payoff a winning bidder earns is the difference between the drawn valuation and the price paid. The price paid by the winner depends on the pricing rule at the auction—whether first or second price. An important difference between an auction and a coin toss is the fact that your behavior at the auction influences the odds that you earn a positive payoff. That is, the probability is not fixed at 50 percent as with a fair coin. Instead, the probability is influenced, at least in part, by how you behave at the auction and is determined entirely by the behavior of all auction participants together. This interdependence is what makes auctions so fascinating to game theorists. As such, equipped with some ideas from game theory and some baseline assumptions that constitute our model, let's explore how bidders should behave at the four types of auctions, assuming the objective is to maximize expected payoffs.

English Auctions

Researchers typically model the English auction as a clock. Like the actual clock often used at Dutch auctions, rather than indicating the time, the metaphorical clock reflects the current price of the object at auction and plays the role of the auctioneer. In an ascending-price setting, imagine that bidders raise their paddles if they are willing to pay the price reported on the clock. Bidders willing to pay higher amounts keep their paddles up, but lower their paddles when the price exceeds what they are willing to pay for the object. The price on the clock rises continuously; as the price ascends, bidders no longer interested in the object lower their paddles. Eventually only two bidders remain active, but the price continues to ascend. When one of those bidders drops out, the clock stops. The winner is the remaining bidder; the price paid is indicated by the clock, specifically, the price at which the last nonwinning bidder left the auction. Economists also refer to this model of an English auction as the *button auction* model: bidders press down on a button as the prices ascends. A bidder releases the button once the price exceeds what he is willing to pay. The last bidder pressing a button is the winner and pays the drop-out price of the last bidder to stop pressing the button.

With this model in mind, how should bidders behave at an English auction? Fortunately, the English auction has a simple solution because each player has a weakly dominant strategy. We encountered the notion of a dominant strategy in our original Prisoners' Dilemma example. There, confessing was a strictly dominant strategy for each player. Strict dominance for Alice meant that regardless of what Bob chose to do, Alice would be strictly better off if she confessed. Weak dominance is just like this, except that it allows for ties. At an English auction, a bidding strategy exists that does at least as well as anything else a given bidder could do, regardless of how rival bidders at the auction behave. Moreover, in at least one instance, this weakly dominant bidding strategy does strictly better than anything else a bidder could have done. Weakly dominant strategies are nice to have—if you're the bidder, it's hard to go wrong. Our claim is that at an English auction each bidder has a weakly dominant strategy to remain active in the auction until the price exceeds the drawn valuation.

Essential to understanding this strategy is recognizing that if a bidder loses the auction then nothing is won—the payoff is zero. With that in mind, a bidder prefers to receive some payoff from winning, provided that the payoff is positive. Because the payoff earned when a bidder wins the auction is the difference between the valuation drawn and the price paid, the bidder should remain active so long as the price is below his valuation—while the difference between them is positive. Once the asking price exceeds a bidder's valuation, however, the payoff becomes negative. Consequently a bidder should remain active whenever the clock reflects a price that is below or at a bidder's valuation, and drop out thereafter. This strategy turns out to provide insight into the second-price, sealed-bid auction—the Vickrey auction—at least within the baseline model.

Vickrey Auctions

What makes the bidding strategy at the English auction so simple to understand is that the increases in the asking price are observed by all bidders—the English auction is an open format. At sealed-bid auctions, bidders have just one chance to tender a bid that is then compared to all the other submitted bids; the object is allocated to the highest bidder, the winning bidder at a Vickrey auction pays the second-highest submitted bid. When bidding at a second-price, sealed-bid auction you are a price taker—the price the winning bidder pays is solely determined by the bids of rivals, and not by any action the winning bidder takes. To be sure, the amount you bid determines *whether* you win, but not what you pay. Consequently, in the baseline model, it is again a weakly dominant strategy for bidders to tender bids that equal their valuations.

Let's investigate this claim formally. When tendering a price, no bidder knows the bids of rivals, so no information concerning the asking price is revealed during the bidding process—the format is closed. To understand the bidding strategy, suppose that a bidder has a valuation of $41, and investigate the potential consequences of bidding something other than $41.

First, consider bidding something less than $41, say, $35. If $35 is the highest bid submitted, then the auction is won and the second-highest submitted bid is paid. For example, suppose that the second-highest bid was $29. Then the difference between the valuation, $41, and the price paid, $29, yields a payoff of $12. Of course, this exact outcome would have obtained had a bid of $41 been tendered as well. If $35 is not the highest bid, then two things can happen: first, suppose that the highest bid is, say, $82, in which case neither a bid of $35 nor one of $41 would have won the object; no harm no foul. The bidder loses the auction in either case and earns nothing. In contrast, imagine the highest bid is something like $39. By submitting a bid of $35, the auction is lost, and the payoff is zero. Tendering $35 leaves our bidder regretting the decision at the close of the auction; improvements could have been made. In particular, had the bidder tendered the valuation $41, then a payoff of $2 would have been earned. Thus bidding less than the drawn valuation can never increase the payoff and will in some cases decrease it.

Next consider bidding something more than $41, say, $44. If $44 is not the highest tender submitted, then the bidder earns nothing—the same amount that would be earned had $41 been bid. Conversely, relative to the case just considered, if $44 is the highest bid, two things can happen: first, if the second-highest bid is $39, then the auction is won with a bid of $44 and also would have been won with a bid of $41; in both cases, a payoff of $2 is earned. However, tendering a bid that exceeds the drawn valuation leaves the bidder open to disappointment. If the second highest bid is $42, and the auction is won with a bid of $44, then the payoff involves a loss of $1. The bidder could have done better by tendering a bid that equaled the drawn valuation. Thus bidding more than the drawn valuation can never increase the payoff and will in some cases decrease it.

Since neither bidding less nor bidding more ever does better, a bidder cannot gain from bidding anything but the drawn valuation. Bidding the drawn valuation is a weakly dominant strategy. Of course, there is nothing special about the number 41 or any of the other arbitrary values in this stylized example.

Another way to think about this strategy is to imagine a seller approaching a bidder with a one-shot, take-it-or-leave-it price offer. A bid at a second-price auction (English or Vickrey, as we have now seen) determines which offers the bidders accept and which offers the bidders reject. A bidder is willing to accept any offers up to the drawn valuation and will walk away from any offers that exceed that value. Although the notion of dominance has allowed us to understand bidder behavior at second-price auctions within the baseline model, such a solution concept is too strong to use when the pricing rule is pay-your-bid.

Pay-Your-Bid Auctions

At first-price auctions the bidding strategy is a bit more complicated than at second-price auctions because the bid you submit determines not only whether you win but also what you must pay if you win. In short, bidding high increases the odds that you win but decreases the payoff if you win; bidding low decreases the odds that you win but increases the payoff if you win. Clearly, a trade-off exists. At second-price auctions, however, your payoff should you win is unaffected by what you bid, so no such trade-off exists.

We focus on the Bayes–Nash equilibrium—the collection of bidding strategies where no bidder wants to deviate, given each player's beliefs about rivals' types and given how rivals behave. Each strategy maps valuations (types) into bids (actions); that is, a strategy prescribes an action the bidder should take for every relevant valuation that bidder might have. This is consistent with what we have been doing so far—at English and Vickrey auctions, the weakly dominant strategy was for bidders to bid their valuation. In a Bayes–Nash equilibrium, each bid function is a best response to the strategies of the other players, given each player's beliefs about rivals.

In trying to maximize expected payoffs, bidders must note that changes to their bids affect their payoffs in two distinct ways: first, the higher the bid a player submits, the lower the payoff earned when the auction is won. No surprise here—a bidder prefers to win with low winning bids as opposed to high winning bids. Second, the higher the bid a player submits, the greater the odds of winning the auction. No surprise here, either. But these two effects go in opposite directions. Finally, an interdependence exists among the bidders—your chances of winning depend not only on your bid, but also on how your bid compares to all the other bids. A strategy that is part of a Bayes–Nash equilibrium reconciles the two trade-offs, for each and every bidder at auction, given the behavior of the other bidders.

A strategy prescribes an action the bidder should take for every relevant valuation that bidder might have.

Although a technical derivation of the Bayes–Nash equilibrium is beyond the scope of this gentle introduction, given the model developed above, some properties of the equilibrium can be understood nonetheless. First, the solution is a symmetric Bayes–Nash equilibrium in which all players adopt the same bidding strategy. Even though we have used the word "symmetric" here, remember that drawn valuations will in general differ across bidders. Thus, even though all bidders are using the same rule to convert a drawn valuation into a bid, submitted bids will differ. Second, players with high valuations bid more than those with low valuations. Third, the bids are *lower than* drawn valuations: bidders shade their bids below their true valuations. In other words, they lie about what the object is worth to them. Moreover those bidders with the high valuations lie more than those with the low valuations. The pricing rule induces this behavior. If players want to earn any positive payoff, then they must ensure that their bids, which reflect the price they will have to pay should they win the auction, are below their private values. The only exception to this rule is a bidder who has drawn the lowest possible valuation. Because every other bidder will have a valuation that exceeds the lowest valuation, this bidder can do no better than to bid the drawn valuation.

Although these properties are somewhat abstract, perhaps we can understand bidder behavior by contrasting it with behavior at second-price auctions. At English and

Vickrey auctions, bidders are price takers. At pay-your-bid auctions, given that bids now determine both whether a bidder wins *and* how much will be paid, bidders are price makers. With this in mind, what exactly does a bid represent? Despite the interdependence among bidders, every bidder is a bit egocentric: given the rules of the auction, the bidder must recognize that the only time payment is required is when the tendered bid is the highest of those submitted. The bidder should think the following: if I submit the highest bid, then this means that I have the highest valuation. If I have the highest valuation, then I have market power, so I do not have to bid my drawn valuation. On average, I just need to beat my nearest opponent, the bidder with the second-highest valuation. Thus I should calculate what I expect the highest valuation of my competitors to be, assuming that their valuations are all less than my own valuation. I can do this because the number of bidders and the properties of the urn of valuations are known to all bidders. I should then tender a bid equal to what I think my most competitive rival's valuation will be, assuming that it is less than my own. When each bidder behaves in this way and tenders a bid equal to this expected amount in equilibrium, no bidder has incentive to deviate from this strategy.

For example, imagine Alice and Bob are the only bidders for an object at auction and that each receives a private value that is randomly drawn from the uniform urn with the lowest possible valuation being zero and the highest one being $100. Recall that, in figure 2, the uniform case is the flat line indicating that the realized valuation of any given bidder has the same chance of occurring in any interval of the same width. Suppose that Alice has drawn the valuation $60. How should she behave at the auction? Following the strategy outlined above, Alice should assume that she has the highest valuation and that Bob's unknown valuation is somewhere between zero and $60. Alice has no information concerning Bob's true valuation other than that it has an equal chance of lying in any interval of fixed length—the probability that Bob's valuation is between $2 and $4 is the same as the probability that his valuation is between $57 and $59 or any other $2 difference you might imagine. Consequently her best guess about Bob's valuation (assuming her own valuation is highest) is the expectation of a uniform random variable distributed evenly between zero and $60. This expectation is the halfway-point of the interval, $30. Therefore Alice should bid $30 at this auction.

This rule holds for any valuation a player might draw and constitutes the Bayes–Nash equilibrium strategy that Alice and Bob should each adopt in this example: each should plan to bid half of her or his valuation. Provided each behaves this way, no player has an incentive to deviate from the strategy. Unlike the strategy at second-price auctions, this prescription is specific to the case of two bidders each having independently and uniformly distributed valuations. The strategy would be different were a different urn used or if, say, another bidder (Charles) also participated at the auction. For example, when Charles also participates, the Bayes–Nash equilibrium strategy is for each bidder (Alice, Bob, and Charles) to tender two-thirds of the drawn valuation. Therefore, if Alice drew the valuation $60 but faced competition from two rivals, then her equilibrium bid would be $40: an increase in the number of rivals means that bidders behave more aggressively, an important lesson. The amount that bidders shade bids relative to valuations decreases as the number of participants at the auction increases because bidders do not consider the expected valuation of a single bidder, but rather the expectation of the largest valuation from the group of rival bidders, which increases with the number of rivals. When more bidders participate at the auction, the odds that one of them has a valuation higher than any given amount increases and the difference between the highest and the second-highest valuation decreases as the number of potential bidders grows.

An important difference exists between what someone would like to do before the auction is held when information is incomplete, and what the same person would do after the auction concludes and the bids have been revealed. For example, suppose that Alice has valuation $60 and Bob has valuation $54 and they are the only two at auction. In equilibrium, Alice should bid $30, while Bob should bid $27. After Alice wins the auction and pays the seller $30, Bob would still be willing to pay up to $54; he is disappointed for having lost the auction. Given Bob did not know at the time he submitted his bid what Alice's valuation was, nor how she would behave, Bob's strategy of bidding $27 is, however, optimal. Certainly, if Bob knew that Alice would bid $27, then he would want to tender a bid of $27.01, but such a strategy ignores the fundamental reason for using an auction in the first place—asymmetric information. Bob does not know Alice's valuation; given all the information he has about Alice, the auction game being played, and the strategy she plays in equilibrium, Bob can do no better than bid half his valuation.

In this same vein, it is important that the rules of the auction be respected. Obviously, after discovering that he has lost the auction, Bob would like to approach the seller, to try to negotiate an agreement whereby Bob would pay the seller something more than the $30, but less than the $54 Bob is willing to pay for the object. Were the seller or the auctioneer to agree to this, they would violate the commitment promised concerning the rules of the auction. In our analysis, we require that the rules of the auction be enforced. At real-world auctions, it is critical that this be done as well. Sellers are bound by the policies they announce *before* bids are received; they cannot change the rules after having seen all of the bids. Naturally a well-functioning legal system is important to the success not just of auctions, but all market institutions. In the absence of a legal system, however, commitment can still play a powerful role, especially when reputation is important. Manipulating the rules after bids are submitted compromises a seller's credibility in all future transactions—severe consequences will follow. Moreover our analysis would be quite different if bidders believed that they could approach the seller with alternative offers after the bids had been submitted and the winner announced. If that were true of most real-world auctions, then the appropriate model is one of bargaining.

Dutch Auctions

Dutch auctions typically involve a clock; these auctions are different in an important way from the metaphoric clock auction used when modeling English auctions. Although the Dutch auction has an open format, the information revealed during the auction is not at all informative to bidders. The only time bidders learn anything from their rivals is when the auction is over: the only action a bidder can take is to stop the clock, which means that bidder is the winner and must pay the price on the clock. Imagine a bidder sitting in a room and participating at a Dutch auction; the bidder is breathless with excitement because the longer the clock goes unstopped, the cheaper will be the object. As the price descends, however, the odds that a rival bidder will stop the clock increase.

The problem faced by a bidder at a Dutch auction is then exactly the same problem as the one faced by a bidder deciding what tender to submit at a first-price, sealed-bid auction. Suppose that the bidder's drawn valuation is the largest among the bidders; the clock should be stopped at the expected value of the next highest valuation, given that valuation is smaller than the bidder's drawn valuation. Put another way, a bidder could write down on a piece of paper the price at which to stop the clock and leave it with the auctioneer who will then follow the instructions. Despite the fact that these two types of auctions are quite different, the Dutch and first-price, sealed-bid auctions are actually the same strategically. Economists refer to these auctions as *strategically equivalent*. Thus everything that we said about behavior at pay-your-bid auctions holds at Dutch auctions as well.

Not only are the first-price, sealed-bid and Dutch auctions strategically equivalent, but within the baseline model English and Vickrey auctions are as well. Thus we can compare bidding behavior across the four types of auctions simply by comparing behavior at sealed-bid auctions under the two pricing rules. Comparing the behavior of bidders at first- and second-price auctions within the baseline model for the case involving two bidders whose valuations are drawn from a uniform distribution over the zero to $100 interval, we depict in figure 3 the bid-ding strategies uncovered in this chapter. The horizontal axis represents a bidder's valuation, while the vertical axis represents the bid that would correspond to each possible valuation. The line labeled "Bid-your-valuation strategy" characterizes behavior at English and Vickrey auctions, while the line labeled "Bid-half-your-valuation strategy" characterizes pay-your-bid and Dutch auctions within this example.

The figure illustrates the notion that a strategy is a rule for mapping types into actions. A bidder could receive any of the valuations depicted on the horizontal axis. To convey a strategy to a proxy bidder before the valuation was drawn, a bidder would simply pass along all of the information contained in one of these lines. Clearly, the difference in the pricing rule (first-price versus second-price) generates important differences in the behavior of bidders at auctions. The bid function at second-price auctions represents a bound on what we can expect from bidders of a certain type. No participant will submit a bid greater than the drawn valuation—the willingness to pay. The bid function at the first-price auction provides you with an example of how the rules of an auction can induce bidders to shade their bids in order to earn a positive expected payoff. The strategies outlined in this chapter hold in the baseline model; if any of the underlying assumptions change, then different predictions of behavior will result. Before we

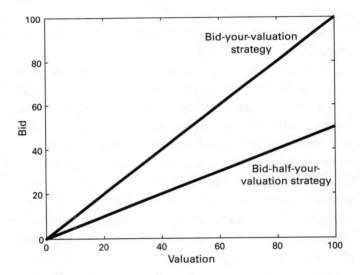

Figure 3 Equilibrium bid functions

relax any of these conditions, however, let's explore some properties of the auction models.

Properties of Outcomes

Auctions are typically conducted for two basic reasons: first, to allocate an object; second, to earn revenue. When it comes to allocating the object, we are interested in the notion of efficiency. Auction researchers consider efficiency in a simple way: did the participant who valued the object the most end up with the object at the conclusion of the auction? Within the baseline model, figure 3 is helpful in demonstrating that all four types of auctions are efficient, provided the seller has no value for the object at auction. The figure demonstrates that bidders with high valuations will submit bids that are greater than those with low valuations. Regardless of the pricing rule, the highest bidder is declared the winner, so all four types of auctions are efficient.

A second reason auctions are used is to generate revenue for the seller. This begs the question: can the seller expect any one of the four types of auctions considered thus far to yield revenues higher than the others? Initially surprising to many, the answer to this question is no. On the one hand, you might think that a first-price auction should yield higher revenues for the seller because the seller receives the highest bid submitted. On the other hand, you might think that a second-price auction should do better because, as we have shown, bidders all tender higher bids in this environment. In the example we depicted in figure 3, bidders all tender bids that are twice as much as what they would submit at a first-price auction. Of course, at a second-price auction, the seller receives the second-highest bid, not the highest bid. Revenue equivalence tells us that, once bidder behavior is internalized, these two factors balance each other out perfectly. In fact this answer generalizes beyond these four types of auctions to any selling mechanism that is efficient in equilibrium and yields a zero expected payoff to the bidder with the lowest possible valuation. This remarkable result, which is referred to as the *revenue equivalence theorem*, is perhaps the most famous result in all of auction theory.

In the interest of full disclosure, let's provide an example of what the revenue equivalence theorem is *not* saying. Imagine that Alice and Bob have valuations of $60 and $54, respectively. Revenue equivalence does not say that a first-price auction and a second-price auction will yield the same selling price. At a second-price auction, Alice will win the object and pay $54, whereas at a first-price auction, if the valuations are generated from a uniform urn, Alice will bid $30 and Bob will bid $27; Alice wins the object and pays her tendered price $30. Clearly, $54 is better for the seller than $30: a second-price auction seems

Revenue equivalence does not say that a first-price auction and a second-price auction will yield the same selling price. ... The relevant comparison is one based on average revenues—in expectation.

better than a first-price auction. In contrast, if Alice has a valuation of $60 and Bob has a valuation of $12, then a second-price auction will now yield revenue of only $12 for the seller, whereas a first-price auction still garners $30 for the seller. Thus you can construct specific examples in which one pricing rule is favored over the other. If Bob had a valuation of $30, then the first- and second-price rules would both yield $30 for the seller, although this is merely a coincidence. All of these examples overlook the fundamental reason for using an auction in the first place—the seller does not know the valuations of either Alice or Bob. Consequently the relevant comparison is one based on average revenues—in expectation. How much does the seller *expect* to receive by conducting the auction according to either first-price or second-price rules? Because the seller is uncertain about the true valuations of Alice and Bob, the revenue equivalence theorem is a powerful result.

To understand revenue equivalence with regard to first- and second-price auctions within the baseline model, think about what bidders at a first-price auction are trying to accomplish. The bidding strategy dictates that players assume they have the highest valuation; given the highest valuation, they tender bids that equal what they expect will be the highest valuation of their rivals. Given that all players behave this way, the highest bid will correspond to the expected second-highest valuation. But that is exactly what the expected price will be at a second-price auction that induces bidders to behave truthfully (bid their valuation) by awarding the object to the highest bidder at the second-highest bid.

Although revenue equivalence ensures that the four types of auctions generate the same revenue, on average, is this the *best* the seller can do? Could the seller change the rules to garner even more revenue? In other words, are these four types of auctions optimal? The seller could do even better than what the baseline model indicates. To see this, let's relax some assumptions of the baseline model by considering alternative rules that the seller could employ and think a bit about potential disparities between our model and real-world auctions.

OTHER ASSUMPTIONS AND RULES

In the typical introductory economics course, students are introduced to competitive markets; initially any form of market intervention that prevents supply from equaling demand is criticized. Adam Smith's advice to leave markets be underlies these prescriptions. According to Smith, the best outcomes for society obtain when economic agents are left to their own devices. This notion is in fact embodied in what is referred to as the *first fundamental theorem of welfare economics*: a competitive equilibrium is efficient; no one can be made better off without making someone else worse off.

To a student new to economics, the first welfare theorem can be depressing: why take any other courses in economics if there is no way to improve overall welfare? Fortunately, later in introductory courses, students learn that when certain conditions do not hold, markets can fail—inefficient outcomes obtain. These situations require economists to guide policy makers, advise firms, and the like.

At this point we can imagine you are probably feeling the same about auctions. The neutrality of the revenue equivalence theorem induces ambivalence; the seller's choice seems unimportant. Fortunately, like those hopeful first-year economics students, you can rest assured knowing that the conditions of the baseline model need not always hold, even approximately. When one of the assumptions is relaxed, it matters which type of auction is used. Of course, this does not mean that the baseline model is wrong, just that it is a model. When constructing models, economists hope to capture the most important features of an environment, but in a simplified way that admits tractability; in other fields, such as computer science, this is referred to as *abstraction*. An economic model can be helpful in making predictions about how economic growth, government policies, reduced trade barriers, technological change, and so forth, will affect the decisions being modeled. A robust model captures the important features of the decision-making process. If, however, for the sake of tractability, certain features have been ignored, then the predictions of the model can be misleading and the value of that model limited.

In the symmetric IPV model, we maintained that risk-neutral bidders drew private valuations of their willingness to pay for an object at auction independently from the same urn. Under these conditions the four types of auctions yield efficient allocations: the participant who values the object the most wins it. The bidder having the lowest possible valuation also receives an expected payoff of zero, and so revenue equivalence obtains.

In this chapter we investigate how relaxing the assumptions required for the revenue equivalence theorem alters the properties of these auctions. In the baseline model many features of real-world auctions that might be important are shut down—ruled out by assumption. We now admit some alternative assumptions that you, too, might have pondered. We use a tool referred to as *comparative statics*: rather than changing many elements of the model all at the same time (which would leave us uncertain concerning why end-results might have changed), we relax one element of the baseline model at a time. This approach highlights the importance of each assumption.

Reserve Price

Returning to our discussion of how sellers must precommit to the rules of the auction, we introduce a new feature, the reserve price—the minimum acceptable bid. With reserve prices, regardless of the auction format or the pricing rule, the highest bid must exceed the minimum acceptable price, otherwise the object goes unsold. At many auctions, sellers impose reserve prices. Why? Before answering this question, note that the reserve price must be set *before* the auction begins and its existence must be made known to all participating at the auction. This rule affects whether an object is awarded as well as the traded price.

For example, outside Dallas, Texas, the Vetro Glass-blowing Studio & Gallery hosts its "Truth or Consequences Auction" each fall. An English auction is used and a particularly dramatic device has been devised to enforce the reserve price. Before the auction, the artist specifies a minimum acceptable price for the glass piece on sale. The glass piece is then placed inside what the auction house calls the "glass guillotine," which is a contraption with metal rods on the bottom and wooden blocks embedded with metal rods that sit a few feet above the object. If the reserve price is not met, then a rope securing the top piece is released allowing the metal to destroy the artwork. Most sellers, however, are not this hard core, but you get the point.

At first-price auctions, the amount a winner pays is unaffected by the reserve price, provided that bid exceeds the minimum acceptable bid. In contrast, at second-price auctions, reserve prices can affect what the winner pays. Recall that the highest bid must exceed the reserve price; otherwise, the seller retains the object. Remember, too, that at these auctions the winning price is determined by the second-highest bid. Therefore the price paid by a winning bidder depends on whether the second-highest bid has exceeded the reserve price. If the second-highest bid is greater than the seller's reserve price, nothing changes; the previous pricing rule is in effect. (Essentially the reserve price is not binding.) If the second-highest bid is less than the seller's reserve price, then the reserve price is binding and the winning bidder must pay the reserve price. Consequently, at a second-price auction, the reserve price can be particularly effective as an insurance device, especially when the seller may receive one high, acceptable bid, but many other low bids.

Given that the second-highest bid determines the price paid by the winner, sellers are rightfully concerned about a sizable difference between the two highest bids; a reserve can be effective in reducing this gap. In 1990 the New Zealand government sold the rights to use electromagnetic spectrum for radio and television as well as mobile phones at auction, but reserve prices were not imposed. To allocate the licenses, the government opted to use the Vickrey auction. Unfortunately, for the government (the seller), unusually low revenues were garnered. One firm bid NZ$100,000 but paid the second-highest bid NZ$6. Another license garnered a high bid of NZ$7,000,000, but the winner only paid NZ$5,000. Some licenses received just one bid; in the absence of a reserve price, those bidders got the licenses for free!

As this discussion suggests, a seller may be able to increase revenue, on average, by employing a reserve price. Clearly, however, a trade-off exists: setting too high a reserve price increases the odds that the object goes unsold but potentially increases the revenues a seller earns when the object is sold. The optimal reserve price balances such trade-offs. Even small reserve prices can yield improvements for the seller as the expected gain from higher selling prices, on average, exceeds the expected loss associated with cases in which the object goes unsold. Thus sellers find it optimal to exclude some bidders from competing at the auction, which is referred to as the *exclusion principle*.

Perhaps surprising to the reader, the optimal reserve price exceeds the seller's own valuation for the object. Until now we have assumed implicitly that the seller does not value the object at auction. In our example, where bidder valuations are evenly distributed between zero and $100, if the seller's valuation is zero, then the optimal reserve price is $50. This corresponds to the highest equilibrium bid at the first-price auction with two bidders when no reserve price exists. The reserve price protects the seller from outcomes in which competition is expected to be low and the bid determining the traded price has a good chance of being low. Essentially the seller uses the reserve price to extract some of the payoff that would otherwise accrue to the winning bidder.

A reserve price of $50 means that, on average, half of the potential bidders will not attend the auction. In our two-bidder example, half the time only one bidder attends, while no one attends one quarter of the time. At second-price auctions, those who participate bid their valuations;

the reserve price provides a backstop preventing low-revenue outcomes. At the first-price auction, those having valuations below $50 do not attend; those having valuations above $50 behave more aggressively because the valuations of rivals who participate are now known to exceed the reserve price. That is, rivals who participate are a self-selected group of bidders having higher-than-average valuations. Because these bidders are willing to pay more on average than those who participate at auctions without a reserve price, all bidders must behave more aggressively at first-price auctions with reserve prices. Thus, when the four types of auctions we have investigated are augmented by an optimal reserve price, the seller's expected revenues can increase. In fact the revenue equivalence theorem generalizes to admit reserve prices. Moreover economic theorists have demonstrated that such auctions are optimal: a seller can expect no higher revenue by using any other auction format, pricing rule, or other modification—such as charging entry fees, requiring payments from multiple bidders, or having multiple rounds of bidding.

From an economist's perspective, the downside of using reserve prices is that the auctions are no longer efficient: in the example above, one quarter of the time the highest-valuation bidder draws a value below the reserve price, and the object goes unsold, which is clearly an inefficient outcome. For example, if Alice has valuation $48 and Bob has valuation $30, both of which were generated from a uniform distribution over zero to $100, then the object will go unsold if the seller imposed a reserve price of $50. This means the object is retained by the seller, who has valuation zero, which is less than what either Alice or Bob was willing to pay for the object. Expected revenue increases, but so too does the chance of an inefficient allocation; this suggests a trade-off may exist between efficiency and revenue.

Our analysis is built on the assumption that the seller publicly announces and commits to a threshold price below which the seller retains the object at auction. In practice, many sellers use secret reserve prices. With a secret reserve price, the bidders understand that a minimum acceptable bid exists, but they are not told its specific value. Christie's and Sotheby's are well known to use secret reserve prices. For example, these auction houses often release expert estimates of low and high prices that a painting is estimated to be worth, but the seller may have a reservation price that differs from either of these estimates and is kept private. Both Christie's and Sotheby's conduct oral, ascending-price auctions—second-price auctions. With or without a reserve price, each bidder still has the incentive to bid his valuation.

At first-price auctions, in the baseline model, no incentive exists for the seller to keep the reserve price hidden as the seller can always do at least as well by publicizing the threshold price as opposed to keeping it hidden. A seller setting a secret reserve price would want to set it equal to the seller's valuation: since it is hidden, there would be no benefit to discarding offers that exceed the seller's valuation at the close of the auction and the object would be worth more to the seller than tenders below her valuation. With an unannounced reserve price, bidder behavior changes solely because those vying for the object know they have to outbid rivals as well as the unknown value to the seller. In some sense, this is like another player is at auction. Still, such a policy does not generate the needed increase in aggressiveness from bidders to outperform an optimally set, publicly announced reserve price, at least in terms of expected revenues. Nevertheless, keeping a reserve price secret may be a good idea in practice; for example, even if a first-price rule is used, when bidders are sufficiently risk averse, having a secret reserve price can improve expected revenues. Similarly, even if a second-price rule is used, but the object at auction has a common value to all participants, then a secret reserve encourages participation. Likewise, if the auctioneer suspects some bidders are colluding, then a secret reserve price may be a way of inducing competition—thwarting collusion. All of these examples require relaxing the assumptions of the baseline model.

Later we will encounter these issues again, but it is important to bear in mind that the seller must be able to commit to this unknown reserve price *before* the bids are revealed. For example, if the seller were to write the reserve price on a piece of paper and place that in a sealed envelope to be opened and revealed to the bidders *after* the tenders have been made, then the seller can precommit to the secret reserve price.

Asymmetric Bidders

If the bidders at auction are inherently different from one another, then the assumption that bidders draw valuations from the same urn is not a good one. Above, we focused on the *symmetric* IPV paradigm. The word symmetric implies that bidders' valuations are drawn from the same urn, a potentially restrictive assumption. If valuations are drawn from different urns, then the model is referred to as *asymmetric*. Asymmetries can arise for any number of reasons. For example, if bidders have different budget constraints, then perhaps the range of feasible valuations is different across bidders. A bidder from Vermont at an auction of an antique tractor in rural New Hampshire faces different costs for transporting the machine back to his property than a farmer from Wisconsin. Transportation costs can impose restrictions on the valuations of the two farmers who might otherwise be considered similar. When a large amount of variation exists in the valuation urn of some bidders, but other bidders face less variation in their urn, private valuations must be modeled differently. Horse owners interested in racing thoroughbreds may have very different valuations, on average, than those interested in breeding thoroughbreds. Of course, there exist other ways in which differences across bidders can be important as well.

When bidders' valuations are drawn from different urns, such differences can change the way bidders behave at auctions. At second-price auctions, however, nothing changes—it remains a weakly dominant strategy for participants to bid their valuations. Outcomes at second-price auctions remain efficient.

On the other hand, at first-price auctions, with asymmetries, the basic rule characterizing equilibrium behavior remains the same: assume you have the highest valuation; choose a bid so that you beat the highest opponent, on average. The difference is that, now, how likely your rivals are to have certain valuations depends on their individual identities because draws are from different urns.

As an example, suppose that Alice and Bob are again bidding at a first-price, sealed-bid auction, but Alice's valuation is equally likely to be between zero and $100, while Bob's is equally likely to be between zero and $50. Even though their valuations are distributed differently, the bidders still understand the relative likelihood of each realizing certain valuations—the distributions are common knowledge. In figure 4, we depict the Bayes–Nash equilibrium bid functions for Alice and Bob in this example as well as their (common) bid function for the case when the two both receive valuations that are drawn from a uniform distribution over the zero to $100 interval. Remember that for the latter, symmetric case we found the first-price equilibrium strategy was for bidders to tender half of their valuation. Thus the symmetric equilibrium bid function is the straight line extending from the point (0, 0) to the point (100, 50).

In this asymmetric example, two functions now exist, one for each bidder: Alice's equilibrium bidding strategy is the one to the southeast that starts leveling off at the end; Bob's is the one to the northwest which continues to rise at the end. Even though the only change from the symmetric example is the way in which Bob's valuations are distributed, both bidders now view their rival as different in a relative sense. As such, both change their behavior in equilibrium compared to the symmetric case. These functions are no longer straight lines; that is completely acceptable. In fact, if anything, the straight-line bid function in the symmetric case is more the exception than the rule. It is no coincidence that the bid-half-your-valuation strategy splits Alice and Bob's bid functions in the asymmetric case. In the asymmetric environment, Bob is now weaker than he was before, so Alice looks relatively stronger. In response to a stronger competitor, Bob realizes that he must bid more aggressively. Likewise Alice's situation

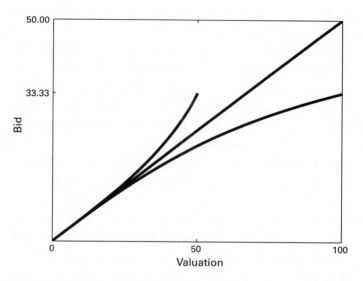

Figure 4   Symmetric/asymmetric bid functions

hasn't changed, but her rival, Bob, now looks like a weaker bidder. Regardless of her valuation, her expectation of Bob's valuation is lower than it was before. Consequently Alice behaves less aggressively. Figure 4 illustrates that for all valuations Alice might receive, her corresponding bid is lower than it was when Bob was a stronger rival. These considerations are mutually consistent and hold in a Bayes–Nash equilibrium.

Instead of comparing how a given bidder changed her/his behavior relative to the symmetric setting, we can also compare behavior across bidders in this asymmetric example. For a given valuation between zero and $50, Bob submits a higher bid than Alice does. This phenomenon is referred to as *weakness breeds aggression*: for the same valuation, the stronger bidder (Alice in our case) does not behave as competitively as the weaker bidder (Bob in our case). Even though every valuation between zero and $50 is feasible for both Alice and Bob, the probability of Bob drawing a type from this interval is greater than it is for Alice. By the definition of our example, Bob *must* draw a valuation in the zero to $50 range, whereas Alice only draws a value within this interval half the time. Thus Alice is a strong bidder, and Bob a weak bidder; for a given valuation, Alice shades her bid by more than Bob does because she has more power. Intuitively, weakness leads to aggression because the bidders are evaluating the likelihood of rivals' receiving valuations that would generate competitive

This phenomenon is referred to as weakness breeds aggression: for the same valuation, the stronger bidder does not behave as competitively as the weaker bidder.

(potentially winning) bids. Weaker bidders need to be more concerned than stronger bidders about rivals having attractive valuations, which prevents them from shading their bids by as much in equilibrium.

Regardless of a bidder's valuation, the bid functions suggest no bidder will ever tender more than $33.33. Were Alice to draw a valuation greater than $50, by tendering a bid at (or just above) $50, Alice could win the auction *with certainty* because Bob can never draw a valuation over $50. Yet Alice never does, choosing instead to never bid more than two-thirds of that amount. This is because Alice is not interested solely in winning every auction at which she competes with Bob; otherwise, bidding her valuation would be a better strategy. Rather, she is interested in maximizing the payoffs she expects to earn, and the pricing rule of a first-price auction means her bid is also responsible for determining the payoff she receives when she wins.

That the highest bid of $33.33 is common to both competitors is interesting, too. To understand this outcome, imagine that Alice bid more than $33.33, say $40. At $40, she will win the auction with certainty because Bob never bids more than $33.33. Thus she could reduce her highest bid to, say, $39 and increase her payoffs when she wins, as she would do so with a lower bid. But then she could reduce that bid and strictly increase her payoffs further. This undercutting story continues until Alice finds herself bidding no more than $33.33. The same argument could be made for Bob were he to bid some amount more than $33.33. In effect, together, these two forces, in equilibrium, bring them to the common high bid of $33.33 (and not some other bid between zero and $50).

When bidders employ different equilibrium bidding strategies, efficiency need no longer obtain. In figure 5 we restrict our plot to the range that is relevant for the asymmetric auction and remove the symmetric equilibrium bid function. We instead identify an instance of an inefficient outcome. In this example, Bob's valuation is $44, while Alice's valuation is $58. Describing how these valuations are mapped into bids is more complicated because the bid functions are nonlinear, so formal equations are needed to characterize equilibrium strategies as opposed to something as simple as "bid-half-your-valuation." Regardless, using their equilibrium bidding strategies, Bob should tender $27.67 when his valuation is $44, while Alice bids $23.99 when her valuation is $58. Since Bob has the highest bid, he wins the auction and pays $27.67. Yet Bob values the object less than Alice does, so the winning allocation is inefficient.

The weakness-breeds-aggression result allows inefficiencies to obtain at first-price auctions. Because the symmetry condition fails, the revenue equivalence theorem no longer holds either. If revenue equivalence no longer holds, then the question of which type of auction will be best for the seller is now an open one. Examples can be

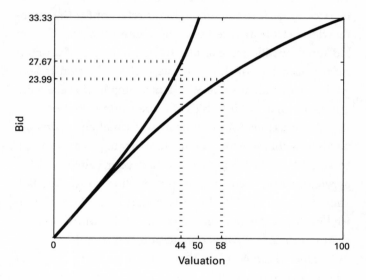

Figure 5 Inefficient outcome

constructed that suggest first-price auctions do better for the seller than second-price auctions, and vice versa. Auction theorists have made some progress in understanding the specific conditions required for each of the urns so that the four types of auctions can be ranked according to expected revenue. Even when those conditions are known, however, understanding which type of auction does better requires understanding the bidders at a given auction.

Risk Aversion

The way valuations are generated for the bidders may seem like something beyond their control. For example, if the underlying motivation of asymmetric urns involves bidders' facing vastly different budget constraints, then the bidders may have little control, at least in the short term. Another way asymmetries can arise is when bidders have different attitudes toward risk. Risk attitudes are something that characterize the bidders' preferences over potential outcomes and imply that the bidders will have different payoffs that reflect their asymmetric preferences. Thus the discussion we had concerning bidder asymmetries can be mapped into one where different attitudes toward risk exist. Rather than reiterate the same points, let's investigate some consequences of relaxing our assumption of risk neutrality by returning to the symmetric IPV model.

Specifically, we maintain that all bidders have the same feelings about uncertain environments, but now they are risk averse.

Attitudes toward risk in no way affect behavior at the second-price auction, either English or Vickrey. Weakly dominant strategies remain and efficient allocations obtain.

Bidders at first-price auctions behave differently. To see why, recall that a risk-averse person would rather accept some lesser amount with certainty than the expected payoff under uncertainty. In the previous coin-flipping example, a risk-averse person might be willing to accept $45 for sure rather than the opportunity to flip a coin and get $100 if it lands heads, but zero if it lands tails. Thus, at pay-your-bid auctions, risk-averse bidders dislike the extreme swings in the payoffs received—winning generates positive payoffs, losing yields nothing. Relative to risk-neutral bidders, risk-averse bidders are willing to accept lower payoffs when they do win (willing to take $45 with certainty) if it means they win more often (reduce the probability of tails—no payment, in the coin-flipping example). Risk-averse players bid more aggressively than risk-neutral ones because they prefer to increase the odds that they receive some payoff at the expense of the size of the payoff they receive: in a Bayes–Nash equilibrium, at a first-price auction, at each valuation, risk-averse bidders tender more than risk-neutral bidders.

Risk-averse players bid more aggressively than risk-neutral ones because they prefer to increase the odds that they receive some payoff at the expense of the size of the payoff they receive.

What does this behavior imply for the revenue a seller can expect to garner at an auction? Well, at second-price auctions, risk-averse bidders behave the same as risk-neutral bidders, so the seller's expected revenue is as before. At first-price auctions, however, risk-averse bidders are all more aggressive than risk-neutral bidders. Thus, on average, at first-price auctions with risk-averse bidders, a seller receives higher revenues than when risk-neutral bidders participate. Since expected revenues at second-price auctions remain the same, while they increase at first-price auctions, a revenue-maximizing seller prefers first-price auctions. First-price auctions with symmetric, risk-averse bidders are also efficient.

All-Pay Auctions

Another fundamental change would involve having losing bidders pay, too. We encountered an example of this in the $10-bill auction discussed in chapter 2. In practice, many auctions require payment from *all* bidders who participate. Sometimes such auctions sound suspicious. Take for example the online auction website QuiBids.com. If you haven't been to QuiBids.com, then you've probably seen advertisements for the website as you browsed around the Internet. Typically these advertisements suggest that you can buy an iPad for less than, say, $40. Sound too good to be true? Let's see how these auctions work.

Quibids.com, DealDash.com, and other websites are often referred to as *penny auctions*, and fall into the general category of what economists refer to as *all-pay* auctions. All-pay auctions involve awarding the object to the highest bidder but requiring payment from all bidders who participate. At the online penny auctions, the auction typically starts at a set time and at a set opening price. Bidders have the opportunity to raise the price by paying a bid fee of, say, $1 that raises the price of the object by a fixed amount that is typically less than the cost of the bid, for example, a dime. The auction ends at a prespecified time or if during some period no bidders have paid the bid fee to increase the price, and thus to position themselves to win the auction. The winner is the last person to have tendered a bid; the winner receives the object for the price at which the auction ended. An example may help illustrate the process.

Imagine an iPad auction that ends with a final price of $40 and that each bid raises the price of the tablet by a dime—10¢. This auction generated $40 \times 10 = 400$ bids, each costing a dollar—so $400, plus the winning bidder must pay the seller $40; the seller garners $440 for the iPad. Of course, the winning bidder pays well under $440 and the actual price depends on the number of bids tendered. The difference between what the seller receives and what the winner pays is funded by the losing bidders.

To maintain the structure of the models we've employed thus far, let's consider an all-pay auction conducted according to a sealed-bid format. In the four common auctions considered up to this point, we did not need to worry about events associated with the probability of losing because the bidders received no payoff. Now, however, even losing requires some payment. If we alter the objective function, then we can again derive the common Bayes–Nash equilibrium bidding strategy employed by bidders in an all-pay, sealed-bid auction. This strategy has many of the same properties alluded to above: if a bidder has a zero valuation, then a bid of zero is tendered. Higher bids are associated with higher valuations. Consequently the all-pay auction is efficient. Because all the assumptions of the baseline model hold and the payment rule is the only thing different, the all-pay auction also satisfies the conditions maintained by the revenue equivalence theorem. In short, for the baseline model the seller can expect the same revenue at an all-pay auction as at the other four types of auctions we examined.

Revenue equivalence can also be used to work backward—to reconcile bidding strategies as well. Because the expected revenue is the same but all bidders must pay now, the winning bidder pays less under the all-pay rule than when only one bidder pays. That is, relative to the first-price auction in the baseline model, bidders will choose to shade their bids by even more at all-pay auctions because payment is required regardless of the outcome. Consequently, as you can see, iPads can sometimes be won online for $40.

All-pay auctions are also a valuable way of selling an object when bidders are interested in the amount of money generated at auction, which is often true for supporters of a charity. At charity auctions, bidders are typically interested in both winning the object and raising money for an organization. If all bidders are interested in helping the organization, then the baseline objective must change to reflect that bidders care not just about their expected payoff concerning whether they win the object but also must reflect that the bidders enjoy seeing the charity raise funds: the revenue equivalence theorem no longer holds in this setting because the bidder with the lowest possible valuation does not get zero expected payoff. In fact that bidder earns a payoff that is linked to the amount of money raised by the charity. Therefore all-pay auctions should generate more revenues than winner-pay auctions if such philanthropic effects are present. Intuitively, at the four types of winner-pay auctions, when rivals outbid each other, the benefits associated with the previous bids are lost, suppressing any incentive to compete. At all-pay auctions, benefits associated with any bids tendered still accrue to the participants, allowing them to ignore such disincentives associated with competitive bidding.

Researchers at Middlebury College conducted auctions both in experimental settings and at real-world fundraising auctions conducted by schools in Vermont and Oregon as well as various Rotary International service clubs throughout the United States. The researchers found that all-pay auctions generate more revenues for charities than winner-pay auctions. In particular, the researchers found strong evidence for charities to raise money by using what they refer to as a *bucket auction*.

The bucket auction works as follows: one randomly selected bidder in the room is given the opportunity to put a nonrefundable chip (which has a fixed monetary value) into a bucket. The bucket is then passed to another bidder in the room who decides whether to place a chip into the bucket. The bucket continues circulating around the room, and the auction ends when no one is willing to place a chip into the bucket. Each time the bucket is passed, those who do not drop a chip are excluded from future rounds. (In that sense the chip is like a per-round ante in Poker.) The bidder who drops the last chip in the bucket is declared the winner. The bucket auction likely plays on a few elements of bidders' emotions: first, they feel good about contributing to the charity; second, because the chips constitute modest payments, bidders can rationalize another small contribution given the amount they have already put into the bucket (something economists refer to as *sunk costs*); third, the bucket can be a great venue for fostering competition among bidders, leading to publicly observed bidding wars. Note that the bucket auction sounds a lot like the online penny auctions we noted above, but bidders have no way of entering the auction late and trying to steal a win having made little-to-no contributions earlier.

Another reason for discussing the all-pay auction is that it illustrates how other situations in the real world can be modeled as auctions, even though they obviously are not. Pfizer Pharmaceutical and Johnson & Johnson spend immense resources trying to discover and to produce new drugs. Research and development departments exist at many firms that expend considerable resources in the pursuit of new innovations and product improvements. Each firm is racing to patent a product first, thus preempting the other from entering the market. Patent holders and first-movers often receive advantages that allow them to be successful relative to rival firms—once one firm has a foothold in a market, its position can become a barrier to entry, making it difficult for rivals (who may have also invested resources) to thrive. Regardless of which firm ends up winning the market, all firms essentially pay their bids—the resources expended in trying to compete for consumers.

The same story can be told about political lobbying by groups or people trying to influence government legislatures and regulatory agencies. Typically those government officials won elections to obtain the positions they hold.

Regardless of which firm ends up winning the market, all firms essentially pay their bids—the resources expended in trying to compete for consumers.

Elections can also be viewed as all-pay auctions in that each candidate spends resources trying to win a seat in office, but only one candidate can hold the seat. Most types of contests can be viewed as all-pay auctions, including sporting events that require team owners to spend money in pursuit of hoisting league championship trophies and hometown parades, even though only one team will have these privileges at the end of a season.

Alternative Models of Valuations

Thus far we have maintained that valuations are inherently specific to each bidder, but some objects are worth the same to all bidders, for example, the jar of coins discussed previously. In that case, bidders differed in their estimates of how much the jar is worth. When the government sells the rights to extract oil from a tract of land, it is very much like selling a jar of coins. Each firm potentially has a different estimate of the odds that oil is present on a given tract of land and, if oil is present, the volume. Such estimates can be informed by experience drilling on nearby tracts, engineers' estimates, and so forth. Regardless, when the oil is extracted, it is sold on international commodity markets at world prices; the extracting firm cannot influence these prices, which are the same to all. The same can be argued for marketable securities, such as treasury bills and bonds. The common-value assumption is in fact appropriate for any object that has a resale value that is unknown to the participants at the time the auction is held.

In the pure common-value model, bidders have different private information (referred to as *signals*) concerning how much the object is worth, but the actual value of the object for sale is the same for everyone.

Differences in bidders' signals generate differences in the bids tendered at auction. If signals that suggest higher estimates of the object's true quality generate higher bids, then because auctions award the object to the highest bidder, a phenomenon referred to as the *winner's curse* is believed to arise. Consider a first-price, sealed-bid auction where the highest bidder is declared the winner, and pays his bid. The winner's curse is so named because the winner receives the "bad" news that winning means that bidder had the most optimistic impression of the object at auction—his estimate of the object's value was higher than those of all other bidders. This feeling of regret becomes worse the larger the number of bidders participating at the auction because, then, the winner's signal was greater than that of a bigger sample of estimates. The winner's curse arises commonly at auctions of jars of coins. The winning bidder is the highest bidder. If the average of all bids approximates the true monetary value of the jar, then the winner will have tendered a bid that exceeds the true value of the coins and will lose money. Some claim that the winner's curse exists at auctions of the right to drill for oil. Others feel that sports teams vying to sign free-agent athletes may find that having bid the most, they have overpaid. (Fans of some teams are notorious for making such claims, regardless of the terms of a player's contract.)

Rational bidders, in equilibrium, should not be so myopic. In equilibrium, bidders employ strategies that embody caution and involve shading their bids below their estimates, mitigating the potential of the winner's curse— even at second-price auctions. Because the regret is greater when more bidders participate at auctions, bidders then shade their bids even more. In revising their bids downward, bidders will not experience a winner's curse by overbidding in equilibrium.

In reality, many objects at auction probably have both private-values and common-value components. A painting can provide aesthetic beauty to buyers with particular preferences, but the painting can also be resold. Indeed many individuals view paintings as investments to be later resold. Thus both private-values and common-value elements may exist. As another example, consider contractors bidding for the right to pave a road in a town. The contractors likely have other ongoing projects, other opportunities to take on future tasks, capacity differences that might constrain how many projects the firms can balance at a given time, and differences in the managerial abilities of the leaders of the firm—in short, features that suggest private values. That said, asphalt is a petroleum-based substance often used in road construction. Consequently all firms are affected in the same way by the price of oil—something none can influence. Likewise the firms competing probably draw labor from the same markets and are subject to the same labor laws and union policies. Thus firm-specific elements as well as those common to all firms influence the costs of completing the project of firms: some dependence in firms' costs exists.

The painting for sale and the road in need of repair suggest that the independent private-values paradigm and the common-value paradigm may be too limiting. These two informational structures belong to a much broader model referred to as the *affiliated-values paradigm*. Several other informational structures within the affiliated-values paradigm exist, which provide connections between the two extremes we have highlighted. Broadly speaking, within the affiliated-values paradigm bidders' valuations (or costs) depend on a common component that has a definite, but unknown value, and an idiosyncratic component which is known to each individual bidder, but unknown to rivals. Thus the affiliated-values model is a general model that allows for dependence across the bidders' valuations.

Affiliation is a very strong form of dependence. In the independent private-values model, a bidder's valuation provides no information concerning the valuations of rivals. When signals are affiliated, observing one bidder's high estimate of the object's true value makes others increase their valuation, too. Such affiliation in bidders' signals and interdependencies in values means the strategic equivalence between English and Vickrey auctions no longer holds. The reason, of course, is the difference in auction formats. In our model of English auctions, active bidders can observe prices at which rival bidders choose to leave the auction (put their paddles down). Because this tells active bidders something about the signals of exiting bidders, those still willing to pay the current asking price can update their estimates of the object's true worth. By construction, the Vickrey auction is closed, so no such information is released to bidders before they tender. Thus, as soon as the assumption that valuations are independent is relaxed, this strategic equivalence breaks down. Pay-your-bid and Dutch auctions remain strategically equivalent because when bids are submitted no difference exists in the information available to bidders concerning the actions of rivals.

Since strategic equivalence no longer holds between the two second-price auctions, it should be no surprise then that the revenue equivalence result breaks down. In fact the auction formats can be ranked according to the expected revenues they can garner for the seller. Specifically, the English auction yields higher expected revenue for the seller than the Vickrey auction, which yields higher expected revenue for the seller than the first-price auctions.

The English auction has the advantage of allowing information to be revealed to bidders as the auction progresses. Bidders can infer information from their rivals' behavior to exit or to remain active at the auction, which mitigates concerns active bidders have about the object's true value. Consequently bidders feel more comfortable in bidding at English auctions than they do at Vickrey auctions where no information is revealed. Of course, the Vickrey auction has in common the advantage (in this case) that bidders are somewhat protected because they pay the second-highest bid submitted. Bidders shade their bids most at first-price auctions for two reasons: first, for the standard reason that they are price makers—the price tendered determines both if a bidder wins the auction and how much the winner pays. Second, bidders want to shield themselves from the winner's curse. In trying to avoid any regret they might feel when the winner is revealed, bidders further shade their bids relative to the baseline model.

This revenue ranking is actually an implication of a broader lesson referred to as the *linkage principle*. The linkage principle states that a seller can expect to increase revenues by providing information to bidders. The linkage principle is the second most famous result in auction theory. When bidders' signals are affiliated and their values interdependent, the payoffs bidders receive due to their private information are reduced if any information relating to the object's value to any of the bidders is publicized.

That is why, for example, the English auction does better for the seller than the Vickrey auction in this setting: bidders can learn about others' private information as the auction is conducted. Consequently the price realized at auction will be more closely aligned with the winning bidder's willingness to pay. The linkage principle means that sellers can improve outcomes if they commit to publicizing information affiliated with bidders' signals—good news or bad. Perhaps this is why we see auctioneers providing bidders with information before the auction is conducted. For example, government agencies often provide engineers' estimates to firms who bid on the right to perform some task. Christie's and Sotheby's list professional estimates of a painting's value in their auction catalogs.

We have relaxed the main elements of the baseline model required for the revenue equivalence theorem to hold and considered alternatives, one at a time, not because we feel that in the real world such combinations are the only ones possible but because doing so allowed us to understand why the assumption is important in the model. These extensions are by no means exhaustive. Certainly auction researchers have constructed models that maintain combinations of the assumptions, which makes theoretical auctions research exciting. Moreover some insights suggested by these models can be undermined by other forces that we have intentionally omitted from our discussion. For example, is full information release still optimal if the auctioneer is concerned that bidders might collude in trying to suppress prices at auction? With that in mind, we use the next two chapters to focus on procurement auctions and Internet auctions, respectively. Such investigations concern auctions that are not just important to our economy but also serve as a way to discuss some of the institutional features concerning how these auctions are conducted in practice, which allows us to continue our discussion of real-world issues.

PROCUREMENT

Procurement is a way of acquiring goods or outsourcing services and tasks that need to be completed, often through a process of competitive bidding. In the US, federal procurement is governed by the Federal Acquisition Regulation, which outlines policies and regulations that nearly all government agencies must follow. In figure 6 we present a graph depicting the trend in US federal spending on contracts from 1990 to 2013. Data for years 1990 to 2003 are from Federal Procurement Reports, while the most recent data are from USAspending.gov. Dollars spent under procurement rose sharply at the turn of the century and peaked with the American Recovery and Reinvestment Act of 2009; the sheer volume of expenditures is enormous, totaling over half a trillion dollars in some years. These data only concern money spent by federal government agencies; state and local governments use procurement as well.

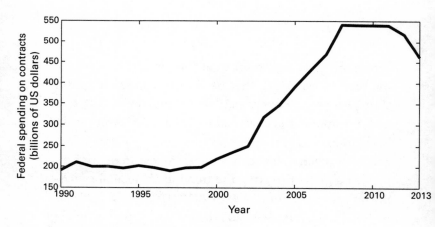

Figure 6 Federal dollars spent on contracts

Procurement auctions, or low-price auctions, are not just used by governments for public purchases but in business-to-business transactions as well. Phrases like "request for proposals" and "call for bids" are now commonplace among employees at firms throughout all industries in the private sector. Other situations can be thought of as Dutch auctions in a low-price setting. An airline with an overbooked flight might continue to raise the compensation package offered to passengers holding tickets until enough passengers have expressed a willingness to be rebooked. A publicly traded company might offer shareholders increasingly higher prices until a target buyback is met.

Researchers typically model procurement auctions as low-price auctions where the contract is awarded to the bidder tendering the lowest bid; that bidder is then paid the amount bid. We use the word contract loosely—this could be an auction at which bidders compete for the right to produce some good for the one buyer (referred to as a *monopsonist*) or to provide some service. Thus our language now shifts to reflect the situation in which bidders, whom we often refer to as firms, have private costs (rather than valuations) and procurers award the task to the bidder tendering the lowest bid. Our discussion of the baseline model and bidder strategies can be adapted to reflect this situation. At second-price auctions, bidders tender their private costs, whereas at first-price auctions bidders submit bids that exceed their costs (just as bidders shade their bids in high-price auctions, these bidders pad their bids). In this chapter we expand our discussion to encompass issues that are not necessarily unique to procurement, but for which the issues are at least prevalent in procurement settings. Many of these issues are in fact common to nearly all auctions, but we use procurement auctions as the vehicle to drive the discussion.

Preparation Costs and Entry Fees

In vying for the right to complete a contract, firms often incur considerable expenses to determine an appropriate bid. Previously we may have given the impression that constructing a bid is a simple task. In fact determining a bid often requires nontrivial resources from firms—either directly in the form of employees responsible for carrying out such tasks, consultants hired to advise the firm, or indirectly in the sense that managers at the firm must allocate time to finding potential opportunities for the firm and gathering needed information in order to assemble a bid.

For example, consider table 4 in which we present the list of bidding items for the California Department of Transportation (Caltrans) contract #10–1C0204 whose project is described as a bridge rehabilitation project. Our goal here is not to wade through each entry of this table.

Instead, what you should note is how specific a contract tender is. This detail is designed to ensure that the government gets what it pays for. To ensure that all bidders have a clear, common understanding of what is required, specific items as well as estimated quantities of these items are presented before the contract is let to firms. The project described in table 4 involves just 35 different items; substantive projects might involve hundreds of lines. In short, interested bidders may need to contact many other firms and suppliers to perform parts of the contract. The firm tendering a bid is referred to as the *prime contractor*, and firms that the prime contractor hires to help with parts of the project are referred to as *subcontractors*. In considering whether to submit a bid, the prime contractor must think about the expenses the firm will incur for all of these items (produced "in-house" or outsourced through subcontractors), consider other commitments the firm will have during the time the project is completed, perhaps think about other contracting opportunities the firm expects will become available, how many employees the firm will need to staff such a project, how far the project is from the firm's headquarters or other job sites, and so forth. All of these factors are at work, of course, in addition to the strategic elements involved with bidding at auction against rival contracting firms.

Sometimes the procurer may also charge an entry fee explicitly—for example, by requiring firms to pay some

Table 4 Project #10–1C0204

Item number	Item code	Item description	Unit of measure	Estimated quantity
1	70030	Lead compliance plan	LS	Lump sum
2	120090	Construction area signs	LS	Lump sum
3	120100	Traffic control system	LS	Lump sum
4	128652	Portable changeable message signs (LS)	LS	Lump sum
5	130100	Job site management	LS	Lump sum
6	130200	Prepare water pollution control program	LS	Lump sum
7	130900	Temporary concrete washout	LS	Lump sum
8	141000	Temporary fence (type ESA)	LF	2,480
9	44649	Remove concrete approach slab surface	SQFT	850
10	153103	Cold plane asphalt concrete pavement	SQYD	490
11	44650	Prepare concrete approach slab surface	SQFT	2,550
12	153227	Furnish polyester concrete overlay	CF	546
13 (F)	153228	Place polyester concrete overlay	SQFT	2,550
14	153531	Access opening, soffit	EA	8
15	157560	Bridge removal (portion)	LS	Lump sum
16	204008	Plant (group H)	EA	36
17	205035	Wood mulch	CY	3
18	390132	Hot mix asphalt (type A)	TON	82
19	480300	Temporary support	LS	Lump sum
20	480400	Temporary decking	LS	Lump sum

Item number	Item code	Item description	Unit of measure	Estimated quantity
21 (F)	510053	Structural concrete, bridge	CY	32
22	511118	Clean expansion joint	LF	90
23	44651	Elastomeric bearing pad	EA	14
24	519091	Joint seal (MR 1 1/2")	LF	90
25	519093	Joint seal assembly (MR 3")	LF	90
26	519098	Joint seal assembly (MR 5 1/2")	LF	90
27 (F)	520102	Bar reinforcing steel (bridge)	LB	2,596
28	820118	Guard railing delineator	EA	4
29	820132	Object marker (type L)	EA	2
30 (F)	833125	Concrete barrier (type 25)	LF	4
31 (F)	833187	Concete barrier (type 27 modified)	LF	4
32	840560	Thermoplastic traffic stripe (sprayable)	LF	950
33	850111	Pavement marker (retroreflective)	EA	17
34	860090	Maintaining existing traffic management system elements during construction	LS	Lump sum
35	999990	Mobilization	LS	Lump sum

amount to obtain the bidding plans. The entry fee can serve to generate funds for the seller, but such fees also reduce participation by potential bidders. In this sense, entry fees have the same effect as reserve prices. Bidders with high costs do not have an incentive to incur the fee and are excluded from the auction in the same way as a reserve price, which in the procurement context represents a maximum amount the monopsonist is willing to pay. In fact, for a given reserve price, a corresponding entry fee exists that can be used to prevent the same set of bidders from entering the auction. An obvious difference exists between the explicit fees charged to bid at an auction and the bid preparation costs that bidders incur in constructing a bid: the former accrue to the seller, while the latter do not.

Each potential bidder at a procurement auction must weigh what the firm anticipates its expected payoff will be from bidding at an auction and compare that to the bid preparation costs. In procurement data, researchers have found that typically fewer than one third of the firms who request official bidding proposals actually end up tendering a bid. Only if the expected payoff from participating exceeds the bid preparation costs will a firm choose to proceed to construct a bid. Thus, as the entry or bid preparation costs increase, fewer bidders participate at the auction.

Interestingly, fundamental implications of the baseline model need not hold in an environment having positive entry costs. For example, if the number of bidders interested in a project increases in the baseline model with no entry cost, all bidders behave more aggressively. In the presence of entry costs, however, two opposing effects obtain. First, as the number of potential bidders increases, holding the entry probability fixed, more bidders

Only if the expected payoff from participating exceeds the bid preparation costs will a firm choose to proceed to construct a bid.

participate at the auction, so bidders become more aggressive, just like in the baseline model. Second, because expected profit must be positive, or at least zero, the entry probability is not fixed as the number of potential bidders increases. Nothing in that trade-off changes when there are more potential bidders: the number of bidders an auction can support remains the same, but as the number of potential bidders increases, the entry probability decreases. Of course, as the entry probability decreases, bidders who do enter the auction behave less aggressively for any fixed number of potential bidders. Whether the first effect, which is often referred to as the *competition effect*, dominates the second effect, often referred to as the *entry effect*, is an empirical question because auction theory does not make a prediction about which effect will dominate. In short, an increase in the number of potential bidders can lead to either an increase or a decrease in expected procurement costs: applied researchers and policy makers must weigh these considerations on a case-by-case basis.

Regardless, one way the procurer can induce potential bidders to participate is to reduce bid-preparation costs. Policies that make it easier for firms to prepare and to submit bids will lower entry costs, which will increase the number of firms who tender bids, which will generate aggressive bidding behavior, which will decrease expected procurement costs.

Collusion

Remember Alice and Bob? The Prisoners' Dilemma arose because each player had a dominant strategy to confess. Even though both would be better off being silent, in equilibrium, they both confessed. If we relabel "Confess" with "Bid Competitive" and "Silent" as "Collude," then the outcome is no longer tragic from the perspective of a seller at auction—competitive bidding ensues in equilibrium. Collusion would involve Alice and Bob cooperating in an attempt to terminate the auction at an inflated price (perhaps negotiating before or after the auction concerning how to divide excess payoffs earned in the process). Such behavior could have the potential to undermine the benefits of the auction process. Moreover collusive behavior can be supported in equilibrium if the game is extended to allow for repeated interactions. The predicted outcome of bidding competitively is only unique if the game is played a finite number of times; that is, the game can be repeated many times, but it is known by players when the game will end. If the game is played repeatedly and indefinitely, and Alice and Bob care enough about future payoffs relative to current payoffs, then the two can employ strategies that allow them to sustain a better outcome. This result is referred to as the *folk theorem* and an application of this theorem suggests that Alice and Bob could collude successfully every time they play the game, provided that a sufficiently high probability exists that the bidders will encounter each other again and the two players do not discount the future, relative to today, by too much. In our auction models, colluding bidders might coordinate their actions explicitly or through informal understandings that aggressive bidding can result in retaliatory bidding wars. Consequently sellers and auctioneers are wise to worry about collusive behavior when bidders encounter each other at auctions repeatedly.

Unfortunately, Tony Soprano wasn't the only one to make his livelihood from rigging bids: many examples of collusion by bidders exist, despite the fact that such behavior violates Section 1 of the Sherman Act concerning antitrust laws and illegal restraints of trade. In fact collusion seems pervasive in auction markets. Bidding rings have existed in state highway construction on Long Island where powerful unions discouraged outside bidders. A former Montreal engineer estimated that Montreal's Italian mafia (known as the "Fabulous Fourteen") controlled 80 percent of the contracts. Consequently road contracts in Quebec have been reported to be nearly 35 percent higher than in other provinces. Collusion has also persisted in the competition for contracts to supply milk to school districts in Florida, Ohio, and Texas. Bidding consortia have been documented in US Forest Service timber sales. Real estate investors in California have admitted to rigging bids at public foreclosure auctions. Investors at municipal tax lien auctions, collectors at stamp auctions, and buyers at cattle auctions have all colluded. These examples highlight the prevalence of bid rigging at many types of auctions.

Perhaps the most blatant slap in the face to auction designers took place openly and in front of the whole world. In 1994 the US Federal Communications Commission (FCC) began selling licenses for the right to provide wireless communication services to customers in specific markets at auctions. These licenses were typically sold for millions of dollars, meaning the difference between a bid of $1,339,011 and one of $1,339,000 was negligible. Because the auction was designed as an ascending-price one where the current high bids were posted after each round and no license was sold until bidding on any license ceased, the trailing digits were used by bidders to communicate through codes. Specifically, the markets were numbered, which allowed bidders to reference licenses openly through the negligible ending digits when submitting their bids. If competition became fierce in one market (say, market number 011), a bidder might outbid a rival on a different license in which it had no genuine interest in acquiring and, in doing so, end their bid with 011 to signal to the rival to avoid further competition for that license. This meant that bids for licenses in Waterloo, Iowa, could be used to suggest that a rival stay away from the Rochester, Minnesota, market. If competition ensued in Rochester, then the agitated bidder might retaliate by outbidding the uncooperative bidder on another license where the firm was currently the high bidder. Thus the firm seeking a license in Rochester could signal to rivals that their day would be made unnecessarily expensive if the firms didn't give up trying to acquire Rochester. Clearly, the FCC was concerned that such behavior dampened the prices paid for these licenses.

Firms that collude or belong to cartels make a concerted effort to reduce competition at the auction in hopes that contracts are won at higher prices. The second-price auction in the baseline model is a good illustrative example. When three bidders participate at the auction, any bidder must outbid two rivals. However, if two bidders form a cartel and decide that one of them will play nicely by ensuring it does not interfere or determine prices at the auction, then the cartel's serious bidder need only beat out one rival bidder. Consequently the cartel bidder can win the contract for a higher price (lower price in a standard auction) on average. At second-price procurement auctions, firms have a weakly dominant strategy to bid their costs. When a cartel member wins, the price is determined by the lowest cost coming from a nonmember firm, something that will be higher, on average, than the second-lowest cost of all firms (including the cartel members). Of course, a bid rotation scheme that showed cartel members participating in auctions only when the other members were not present would surely raise flags with the auctioneer. Instead, the other cartel members typically submit nonserious tenders (which are often referred to as *phantom bids*) that ensure the contract is won at a price that is not lower than were these firms absent from the auction but also prevents easy detection of the cartel's operation.

Although such outcomes are clearly in the interest of the winning bidder, what incentives do the other firms have to abide by the collusive agreement? How does the cartel decide which firm should be the serious bidder? These two questions can actually be answered by applying what we have learned. The cartel faces a problem: the true costs of its members are unknown. Thus, to determine which member firm has the best shot of winning the auction, use a mock auction before the real auction! Researchers refer to this mock auction as the *preauction knockout* auction. Imagine that the preauction knockout auction is conducted using the second-price format. The firm with the lowest cost wins the preauction knockout (ensuring efficiency) and represents the cartel at the real auction. The winning preauction knockout price is recorded and the nonwinning members agree to submit phantom bids at the real auction. At the real auction, if the cartel's serious bidder wins the auction, then that firm agrees to pay the cartel the difference between the price at which the firm won the real auction and the price determined in the preauction knockout. The difference paid represents the price the firm would have paid if the cartel were dissolved and all firms bid honestly. This payment can then be shared among the cartel members.

Because the preauction knockout is efficient, no cartel member has an incentive to displace the prescribed winner at the real auction. By comparison, the incentives to follow the agreement of a cartel that competes at first-price auctions are a bit tenuous. At first-price auctions, bidders' tenders are greater than costs. Nonserious bidders may be tempted to behave more aggressively in hopes of winning the contract if the expected payoff from doing so outweighs the value of remaining a cartel member; this depends on how the cartel punishes cheaters. Tony Soprano did not have problems, but others might.

For a cartel to be successful, members must be able to identify firms that cheat on any agreement and then punish them. Aiding detection would be the release of information concerning behavior at an auction. This means that open-format auctions where the bidders can observe directly the behavior of other bidders actually serve as a way for a cartel to monitor its members. Sealed-bid auctions prevent detection from taking place during the auction.

We have paid little attention to what information is provided to bidders after an auction is complete, but the information that is publicized can be important when bidders encounter one another repeatedly. After some auctions, just the winning bid is released. After others, both the winning bid and the identity of the winning firm are made known. After yet others, all bids and the identity of the winner are released. Finally, in some settings, all bids are released as well as the identities of the firms tendering those bids. In an effort to be transparent and to demonstrate that contracts are awarded fairly, most governments release details concerning all bids tendered. For example, when the contract specified in table 4 was allocated, Caltrans published all firms' total bids (which were used to make the awarding decision) as well as the cost each firm suggested would be required for each of the 35 items. From a cartel's perspective, however, more information is better because it makes identifying cheating easy. Thus the government's policy of transparency also makes the auctions susceptible to collusion. If firms that are ring members of a cartel do not abide by the agreement, they will be exposed immediately following the auction. These firms then have less incentive to take actions (such as bidding competitively) that go against the cartel's plan in fear of immediate repercussions. Consequently information released concerning past auctions allows cartels to detect cheating members and serves as a way to ensure that punishments are meted out.

What can the buyer do to mitigate collusion, yet still maintain the integrity of the procurement process? Anything the buyer can do to make firms rethink their actions will help. Likewise the buyer should not help the cartel in its mission—the less information released during or after the auction the better. This could mean avoiding open formats and favoring closed ones. First-price auctions can disrupt the incentives of members to remain loyal to the bidding ring. Of course, this advice goes against the prescription of releasing lots of information at auctions when bidders have affiliated valuations. When firms collude, it's as if the colluding members behave jointly as one bidder in hopes that reduced competition will allow the contract to be won for a higher price (lower price in our standard, non-procurement setting). To combat this, a more stringent reserve price must be used—in the procurement setting this means reducing the maximum amount the seller is willing to pay, whereas in the high-price setting this means raising the minimum acceptable bid. The reserve price that is optimal will be lower (higher) in the procurement (standard) setting than what a seller would use in the absence of collusion and will be decreasing (increasing) as the number of colluding firms increases. The reserve price serves as a way of mitigating the effectiveness of a cartel.

Such policies can be very contentious. For example, striking oil workers were met with riot police firing tear gas and rubber bullets in Rio de Janeiro in the fall of 2013 after a group of five firms formed a consortium and tendered the lone bid, the lowest possible to win the rights to explore Brazil's biggest oilfield despite interest from a dozen bidders. Although protesters might have been concerned about the government allowing the rights to explore the Libra field at too low of a price, government officials characterized the auction as a success.

Unfortunately, preventing and detecting collusion at auctions is not easy. The Department of Justice in fact posts this plea on its website describing the most common antitrust violations "These conspiracies are by their nature secret and difficult to detect. The Antitrust Division needs your help in uncovering them and bringing them to our attention."

Scoring Auctions

Thus far we have considered auctions at which the rule determining the winning bidder is one-dimensional: price is the only thing that mattered. The pricing rule of the auction can sometimes be used to reflect other considerations that might be important to the seller. For example, consider the average bid auction used by the Italian government and described in chapter 1. The government discarded the highest and lowest offers and determined the winning firm by the proximity of its bid relative to an average of the other bids. This nonstandard pricing rule may have served as a way to screen offers that are unreliable—too good to be true. If the most attractive offers regularly require the awarding agency to renegotiate terms with the winning firm, then the average bid auction might provide a better representation of the cost to complete a project, allowing the agency to avoid post-auction transaction costs. Remember, however, that price is already doing a lot of heavy lifting, especially at procurement auctions—it serves to determine both to whom the contract is awarded and what associated payment will be made.

Procurers may consider other factors when awarding contracts, perhaps because they have objectives other than reducing costs (or raising funds). Even though price is still important, it is not all important. For example, a municipality may wish to consider the time that would be required for a contractor to reconstruct a bridge because closing the bridge for repair will affect traffic patterns and cause delays, thus inconveniencing commuters. A university constructing a new building on campus may be interested in a green design; it might care that the wood used in construction is certified to meet ecological criteria, has a sufficient share of recycled content, or employs a particular wastewater technology. Of course, minimum standards concerning the quality of materials to be used, the maximum number of days for work to be completed, acceptable project work hours, and so forth, can be stated when the contract is posted. Instead, it may be optimal to be flexible along these dimensions, and to convey to bidders that such criteria matter in awarding the contract. Auction researchers refer to auctions at which the determination of the winning bidder is a multidimensional rule as *scoring auctions* or, when the rule combines elements linearly, *A+B auctions*. These auctions are attractive because they admit trade-offs involving features like design or how a contract will be carried out, but maintain the competitive aspect of auctions, which can help in achieving lower prices—especially if alternatives like bargaining involve one-shot negotiation with each contractor and not a back-and-forth in which their offers are played off each other, something that may be impossible given time constraints.

Broadly speaking, the buyer will likely consider how good of a match the bidding firms' products are with the government's needs along a number of attributes. If you've used TaskRabbit (at least prior to July of 2014), you have likely had some experience in evaluating offers on considerations other than price. TaskRabbit allows people to post jobs they'd like to have others complete for them and a (hidden) maximum price that they would be willing to pay—again, think of this a reserve price in a setting where low bids are desired. Once bids are collected, however, the task-poster need not award the contract to the lowest bidder. Rather, the poster can review all tenders and choose which rabbit is awarded the job. Importantly, the experience, reviews received by the various rabbits, or level (ranking) each rabbit has attained can drive the poster's decision over who gets awarded the task. Economists often refer to auctions like the TaskRabbit auction as *beauty contests* because the buyer reviews offers along many dimensions, but how the award choice is determined is not explicitly stated to bidders beforehand. In short, beauty contests do not involve precommitment.

Private commercial and residential procurement projects often employ such mechanisms. Moreover, although consumers typically purchase finished products, many transactions exist throughout the supply chain that are rarely performed single-handedly by an individual firm. Throughout the production process, firms interact upstream, downstream, and horizontally with other firms throughout the supply chain. We can think of these relationships as business-to-business (B2B) commerce. Not surprisingly, the Internet has opened up the ways businesses conduct business with each other. B2B procurement auctions can be thought of as situations where various, perhaps, differentiated products are proposed and the purchasing firm makes a decision that is based not just on the price it must pay but also on the "match" of the sellers' products.

The distinction between scoring auctions and beauty contests is whether the rule determining contract award is spelled out clearly to bidders beforehand. In B2B transactions, there are situations where each is likely to be used. We will maintain our focus on government procurement, which is often required by law to be transparent in soliciting bids, determining a winner, and reporting results, meaning the procurer is typically bound to presenting bidders with a rule and then abiding by it in making the award decision. Thus scoring auctions can be thought of as a mechanism in which the salient elements, as determined by the procurer, are mapped into an index according to a formal rule, which can then be used to rank the offers and determine a winner. Consider a simple scoring rule that is often employed throughout the country: bid preference policies.

Bid preference policies are scoring rules based on the price tendered by each firm as well as the firm's eligibility to receive preferential treatment. By making the preference policy explicit, these two factors are then used to generate a score. Many public procuring agencies are often interested in either maintaining or increasing the role certain classes of firms play in the tendering process. For example, the Buy American Act of 1933 specifies that the federal government favor American-made products in its purchases. The State of California grants a 5 percent preference to certified small business. The City of Tucson allows minority and woman-owned firms to receive between 5 and 7 percent preference on city construction projects. Contracting firms regularly receive benefits if the majority owner is a veteran or is disabled. Braulio Castillo's firm won nearly half a billion dollars' worth of contracts with the Internal Revenue Service, after qualifying for preferential treatment given his firm's status as a "service-disabled, veteran-owned small business." Congresswoman Tammy Duckworth, who lost both her legs during the Iraq war, chastised Castillo during a House Oversight and Government Reform Committee hearing in 2013 for claiming such status due to an ankle injury sustained while playing sports at a military prep school. Her dramatic questioning of Castillo made clear the extreme measures sometimes taken to receive such classifications. These examples demonstrate that such policies are ubiquitous at all levels of government and for many types of firms.

To understand the mechanics and subtleties of bid preference policies, consider an example in which Alice and Bob each own a firm and are the only two vying for the right to complete a contract. Imagine the awarding agency specifies beforehand that Alice's firm will receive a 5 percent bid preference for the purposes of evaluation. Let's suppose that Alice tenders a bid of $104.99 while Bob submits a bid of $100. At a standard (nonpreference) procurement auction, Bob would be the lowest bidder and would win the contract, being paid $100 for doing so. With the preference rule, the prices submitted must be combined with the preference eligibility and mapped into scores. Bob does not qualify so his score remains at 100. Alice, however, receives a 5 percent preference so her score is actually $104.99 \div 1.05 = 99.99$. In this procurement case, where the low score wins, Alice now has a lower score and is awarded the contract.

Although we remain agnostic about why the government might want to employ these policies, you can at least understand the benefits and costs of them. Critics of bid preference policies might use this example with Alice and Bob to demonstrate one consequence of such policies: the scoring rule is used to determine who wins, but the winner is still paid what was bid. In this case Alice is compensated for what she actually bid, which was $104.99; in contrast, without the preference policy, Bob would be awarded the contract and paid only $100. A $4.99 difference exists: does such a policy mean increased cost to the government and thus taxpayer? Won't the outcome be inefficient? The latter question can be considered by recalling how inefficiencies might arise in the presence of asymmetries. Whereas in our earlier presentation an asymmetry was introduced by having bidders draw valuations from different distributions, here an asymmetry obtains even if costs are drawn from the same distribution. Why? Because the scoring rule means that bidders of distinct classes will behave differently in equilibrium; thus the potential for inefficient allocations exists. Of course, recognizing bidders behave differently is also the key to addressing (or at least evaluating appropriately) the critic's concern about cost as well.

Bidder behavior, relative to the baseline model, can change in important ways. Nonpreferred bidders like Bob will behave more aggressively when rivals receive preferential treatment, tendering lower markups relative to the price-only case. Preferred bidders like Alice may inflate bids associated with certain cost realizations because a given score can be secured with a higher bid when the preference rate is positive. Consequently, it seems, the cost to the government may be higher or lower with the preference rule than in the absence of the policy. Finally, the preference rule can induce different participation rates from firms belonging to the preferred and nonpreferred classes. Changes in the number of bidders at auction will be an important factor in determining how expected cost changes. The overall effect on the procurer will depend on the magnitudes and aggregation of these effects. Although researchers have derived conditions under which the change in expected cost can be signed, it is largely a question that depends on the specific situation under consideration. This is not a very satisfying answer, but it makes for exciting research and demonstrates a deeper lesson: nearly all auction settings require custom-made policy advice based on the object being bought or sold, preferences of the seller, characteristics of the bidders, and environment in which the auction is conducted. Regardless, the bid preference policy allows us to think about how bidder incentives change within the context of a scoring setting.

It is worth exploring one more subtlety related to bidder incentives at auction when bidders are essentially given choices over how to formulate bids. The public-private auction relationship is not just a one-way street. Although we

Nearly all auction settings require custom-made policy advice based on the object being bought or sold, preferences of the seller, characteristics of the bidders, and environment in which the auction is conducted.

have focused on situations in which the government contracts firms to complete tasks for which checks are written to the firms, the government also provides firms with opportunities to earn income and asks for a piece of the pie. A good example is timber: firms that promise to compensate the government the most for stems harvested are given the right to fell designated timber. If you've walked through any wooded trail you realize quickly the diversity of species growing on a tract of land. An American Red Oak and an Eastern White Pine of the same dimension mean different things to the harvesting firm because the former is a hardwood and the latter a softwood. Thus, to conduct these auctions, the relevant forest service department estimates the quantity of each species and asks firms to bid a per-unit price for each species. Consequently these auctions are often referred to as *unit-price auctions*. These per-unit prices are what the firms promise the government, for each stem of the relevant species harvested. The winning firm is the one with the highest computed score, which is determined by summing the product of the per-unit price bid by each firm with the government-reported estimate of each species. This simple scoring rule weights highly species that the government estimates will be the most prevalent.

Timber auctions conducted according to this aggregated score open the door to some interesting behavior by firms. Two other aspects of these auctions are also worth noting: first, firms are allowed to do their own homework; that is, they can cruise the tract for themselves to understand its composition better. Second, although the winner is the firm with the highest score, the amount the winning firm pays the government is based on what is actually scaled from the forest. Differences between the government estimate and the firm's private belief about the composition imply that firms can manipulate their bids in ways that increases their chances of winning the auction, but decrease the payment it anticipates making, relative to what its bid suggested. To do this, the firm can skew its bid on species it believes have been overstated in the government estimate, which is in part driving the scoring rule. For example, imagine a simple tract that the government estimates is comprised equally of red oak and white pine trees. A bid from a firm of $100 per red oak and $100 per white pine mean the average bid is $100. If the firm believes the tract actually has 55 percent red oak and 45 percent white pine, then the firm expects to pay $100 using that bid as well. But what if the firm skewed its bid on white pines, which it feels has been overestimated? Suppose that the firm bid $60 per red oak and $140 per white pine. In that case the firm's bid would be equally as competitive as $100 for either species, but the firm would expect to pay only $96 on average.

Bid skewing is consistent with how theory predicts bidders should behave in equilibrium. Bidders with estimates most different from the government estimate will distort their bids the most. Unfortunately, this opens the door to inefficiencies because bids are influenced not just by actual costs, but also by strategic skewing. Although the government's scoring rule and payment plan allows for risk sharing and protects bidders against disparities between the estimate and the actual volume harvested, a role for policy makers exists. One option could be to change the auction format, for example, a lump-sum sale of the right to harvest all timber in which winners make a one-time (much larger!) payment to the government.

A less extreme alternative would be to limit the amount of skewing allowed. This is what is typically done in procurement contracting. Many procuring agencies compute the total bid by summing up the bids on individual contract components. For example, in the last two columns of table 4 which concerned the bridge rehabilitation project in California, the contract specified estimated quantities. If firms believe these quantities are off and if payment will depend on actual quantities used, then firms can skew their bids to exploit such discrepancies. In the procurement setting, firms can benefit by increasing prices on items they expect to need more of and decreasing prices on items that it feels have been overestimated. As a solution, government agencies might protect against such behavior by requiring a renegotiation of the unit price if the actual quantities are sufficiently different from the estimated ones. This solution also has the advantage over a lump-sum price in that renegotiation can be done more easily if each component of a contract has been priced beforehand. Because procurement contracts are often incomplete, after the winning bidder has been declared, initial plans must be changed and refinements made. You need only look to the "Big Dig" in Boston to understand how complicated projects can become if conditions differ from expectations. It turns out that such adaptation and transaction costs can be quite large relative to the amounts by which firms mark up their prices over costs. Although these costs are large, trying to avoid them is a slippery slope. For unique projects, engaging firms in a design-build-type framework where a single construction firm is contracted to propose and to complete a project could challenge the advantage that competitive bidding serves to limit favoritism as well as the influence of political ties.

With many managers looking for the best economic value rather than just the lowest price for doing something, and nearly all US states and the European Union allowing for and, in some cases, mandating scoring auctions for public procurement, understanding them is critical. Economists know that provided that the scoring rule involves adding bids (or a multiplicative factor of them) to other elements, and provided that no dependence in firms' costs exist, then even if firms have private information concerning many different cost factors, characterizing equilibrium behavior is analogous to the standard procurement model we have described. Essentially, in such settings, it is possible to collapse the multidimensional private information into a single number that plays a role akin to the realized private cost we discussed in the models earlier. Thus, for a general class of scoring rules, a correspondence has been established between scoring auctions and the standard IPV auctions. Nevertheless, as the bid preferences and unit-price examples suggest, subtleties are important, especially in these complex settings.

In this chapter, we used procurement to introduce some other features of auctions. In the next chapter, we use Internet auctions to explore features that are relevant to virtual environments.

INTERNET AUCTIONS

Three years before Tom Hanks and Meg Ryan again joined forces in *You've Got Mail*, Pierre Omidyar was running the auction website AuctionWeb, out of a house in Silicon Valley. By the time *You've Got Mail* hit the big screen, Omidyar was a billionaire, after his company, renamed eBay, went public. At that time, eBay's growth exceeded 1,000 percent per quarter.

eBay made people independent by connecting them to the rest of the world, or at least the part that had access to the Internet. One core lesson of auction theory is that the seller can expect higher prices for an object that bidders value privately when the number of bidders at the auction increases. By connecting bidders virtually, eBay expanded the number of potential bidders, thus allowing sellers to garner higher prices.

Perhaps better than any other auction market, however, eBay epitomizes the notion that auctions can be used to discover the price of unique objects. Some quirky examples of things sold on eBay (with winning prices noted in parentheses) include a cornflake shaped like the state of Illinois ($1,350), the oldest known pair of Levi jeans ($46,532), lunch with Warren Buffet ($2.63 million), a tissue used by Scarlett Johansen on *The Tonight Show with Jay Leno* ($5,300), a handwritten letter from Albert Einstein to Erik Gutkind ($3 million), a piece of the Zagami Martian meteorite ($450,000), and the town of Albert, Texas ($2.5 million). Although unsuccessful, sellers have also used eBay as a venue to try to sell a grandmother, personal organs, the telephone number made famous by Tommy Tutone (867–5309 with various area codes), military fighter jets, and a ghost in a jar. eBay has made a reality of the expression "one man's junk is another man's treasure." As mentioned, legend has it that Omidyar himself sold the first such object on eBay—a broken laser pointer.

Websites like eBay provide what economists refer to as *network effects*. The value of the online marketplace is greater to an individual participant the more participants are involved: buyers benefit from a large number of sellers making it more likely that they can find items that interest them; sellers benefit from a large number of buyers because competition increases average traded prices. Such network effects make it difficult for new online auction websites to enter the industry. Consequently, eBay remains the dominant Internet auction. Nevertheless,

The value of the
online marketplace is
greater to an individual
participant the more
participants are
involved.

online auctions have proliferated in other parts of the economy. For example, Goodwill Industries sells objects at auctions on ShopGoodwill.com using the proceeds to support its missions; PropertyRoom.com sells goods seized by law enforcement officers at auction; the money goes back to communities across the United States; GovDeals.com, GovSales.gov, and PublicSurplus.com permit various government agencies to sell surplus items, confiscated goods, even real estate, at auction; uBid.com works with preapproved, authorized merchants to auction refurbished and overstocked items. Because Internet auctions are now a staple in today's economy, exploring auction-related issues in these virtual settings is obviously important.

eBay's Pricing Rule

Electronic auctions, such as those implemented by eBay, have some features in common with the four types of auctions already investigated, but others that make them unique. In common with English auctions, Internet auctions have bid increments. A bid increment is the minimum amount that one bid must exceed another. In the open-auction formats considered earlier, we ignored any discreteness in how prices are formed. The clock model avoided large jumps in price; several bidders could not exit the auction at the same time, which ensured that bids corresponded exactly to the predictions of the model. Of course, this clock model eliminates features that can be important—for instance, in practice, auctioneers at English auctions either formally or informally use bid increments of fixed values. In such cases the auctioneer may call out a price that exceeds the price the second-highest bidder would be willing to pay, but is less than what the highest bidder is willing to pay. Alternatively, two bidders might be willing to pay the current price, but the object is awarded to whomever is recognized as the leading bidder simply because the price that gets subsequently called out (which includes a bid increment) exceeds both bidders' willingness to pay. Clearly, bid increments have the potential to generate inefficiencies at auctions.

The bid increments used by eBay follow a formal schedule that varies with the current price of the object at auction; in table 5, we report the bid-increment schedule used on eBay. The first two columns describe the range of the current price and the third column specifies the bid increment. For example, for an object priced between $25 and $99.99, the bid increment will be $1. The last two columns show the bid increment as a percentage of the prices listed in the first two columns. Typically, as the asking price increases, the relative bid increment falls to between 1 and 2 percent of the high and low prices, respectively.

Another aspect ignored in the clock model is the ability of bidders to call out offers; economists refer to these as

Table 5 Bid increment schedule used by eBay

Low price ($)	High price ($)	Bid increment ($)	Increment/ low price (%)	Increment/ high price (%)
0.01	0.99	0.05	500	5
1.00	4.99	0.25	25	5
5.00	24.99	0.50	10	2
25.00	99.99	1.00	4	1
100.00	249.99	2.50	2.5	1
250.00	499.99	5.00	2	1
500.00	999.99	10.00	2	1
1,000.00	2499.99	25.00	2.5	1
2,500.00	4999.99	50.00	2	1
5,000.00		100.00	2	–

jump bids. Jump bids are bidder initiated and may deviate from any schedule an auctioneer uses to increase the asking price. The baseline model can be adapted to reflect bidders who might be impatient or who have a time cost that induces such behavior. Likewise behavioral considerations can be important: bidders may see jump bidding as a form of strategic intimidation.

At Internet auctions, bidding typically takes place using a procedure referred to as *proxy bidding*: a bidder reports a number to a website server that represents the most that bidder is willing to pay for the object at auction. The number reported is unknown to rivals, but it permits the bidder to authorize the server to act on the bidder's behalf.

Because Internet auctions are typically conducted over days, the proxy removes the need of the bidder to monitor the auction closely; the server does all the work—tendering values that exceed rival bids and notifying the bidder when the current price exceeds the authorized threshold. eBay tries to induce truth-telling on the part of bidders by making the current price equal to the second-highest price submitted, plus the bid increment, rather than the value of the highest proxy bid tendered. This means that eBay's proxy-bid server performs buyer-friendly jump bids. The asking price is not tied to any formal schedule of an eBay auctioneer, but rather the price is permitted to increase by amounts that make the bidder with the highest proxy bid the standing bidder, but at the lowest possible price given the bid increment and second-highest bid.

For instance, consider a situation where the current asking price is $10. Suppose that Alice and Bob tender proxy bids of $35 and $50, respectively, which exceed the proxy bids of all other rivals. eBay will list Bob as the current high bidder and put the current asking price at $36—since $35 is the next-highest bid and the bid increment is $1. Thus, because the price does not rise until bidders explicitly force price increases that exceed the current asking price, the eBay auction is quasi-open. Proxy bids can act like jump bids at an English auction. With that in mind, the proxy bidding stage of the auction can be thought of as sealed-bid, so the eBay auction is also very close to a

Vickrey auction. Although the English and Vickrey auctions are both second-price auctions, Internet auctions actually possess first-price elements as well.

Consider an eBay auction for a pair of Ray-Ban sunglasses. The standard listing shows the current high bid, the number of bids tendered thus far, and the minimum amount required of a new bid. Information on the item, the seller, as well as the shipping, payment, returns, and guarantee policies involved are also provided. Suppose that the current price of the sunglasses is $117.50. Then the smallest possible new bid a buyer could tender is $120.00, which is deduced from the current bid of $117.50 plus the $2.50 bid increment. The highest proxy could be greater than $120.00, in which case a bidder who enters $120.00 successfully enters the auction but is soon overtaken by a rival through the proxy server. If the highest proxy bid tendered is between $117.50 and $119.99, a bid of $120.00 would put the next bidder in a position to win the auction.

This last consideration uncovers an interesting complication. Bid increments clash with the proxy system when the difference between the highest tendered proxy bid and the current asking price is less than the required bid increment. eBay faces a decision: either award the object to the bidder tendering the highest price but ignore the bid increment schedule or maintain the bid schedule and keep the current (lower) price. Consistent with the auctions we've examined, eBay opts for the former and decides the highest bidder should be the winner. Since the price submitted to the proxy system exceeds the current bid by less than the bid increment, eBay charges the bidder exactly the tendered proxy bid—as if eBay were a first-price auction. Therefore the pricing rule at eBay auctions is neither a pure second-price nor a pure first-price auction: because the second-price (plus bid increment) rule holds in some cases, while the first-price rule holds in others, the eBay pricing rule is a hybrid of the two. This change in the pricing rule changes equilibrium bidder behavior. In short, truth-telling is not an equilibrium at an eBay auction. In fact, because there is a chance that the winner pays her/his bid, in equilibrium, eBay bidders should shade bids, but not by as much as at an auction where the pricing rule dictates that a first-price rule is always used.

Sniping

At an English auction, the auctioneer typically encourages bidding to continue until no one is willing to bid higher than the standing price. To warn rivals that the auction could be near its end, the auctioneer often employs language like "Going once, going twice, sold!" or "Going, going, gone!" before the object is knocked down. These cues provide final opportunities to prolong the auction. Under this convention all bidders know they will be given the same courtesy warning should they not be the current high bidder—that is, the object will not be awarded at a price that is less than what they are willing to pay.

Many online auctions end at a fixed point in time. For example, on eBay, sellers have the option of conducting auctions that last one, three, five, seven, or ten days. Regardless of the duration chosen by the seller, the auction ends at a fixed point in time. Under these rules bidders may have an incentive to engage in *sniping*. Sniping involves tendering a bid just before the close of an auction—to prevent rivals from responding. Software like Bidnapper, Auction Sniper, AuctionStealer, eSnipe, and EZsniper exist specifically to support this behavior, suggesting that eBay participants believe the tactic is valuable.

Why do bidders snipe? To prevent bidding wars that might ensue were bids tendered earlier at the auction, leaving rivals the chance to respond, is one explanation. In short, sniping is a defense against incremental bidders who might try to monitor the auction manually to maintain their status as high bidder. Let's return to the eBay auction of the pair of Ray-Bans (the information provided is from an actual eBay auction for Wayfarer sunglasses, although we use pseudonyms in our presentation). Participants can view the bid history at any point during the auction by clicking a link on the listing page. Doing so yields the information provided in table 6. Four unique bidders participated, but seven bids have been tendered—Charles

Table 6 Bid history for Wayfarers

Bidders: 4 **Bids**: 7 **Time left**: 1 hour 22 mins 51 secs **Duration**: 7 days

Only actual bids (not automatic bids generated up to a bidder's maximum) are shown. Automatic bids may be placed days or hours before a listing ends.

Show automatic bids

Bidder	Bid amount	Bid time
Charles (4)	**US $117.50**	**Jun-21–14 17:31:42 PDT**
Danielle (87 ★)	US $115.00	Jun-18–14 13:34:39 PDT
Charles (4)	US $113.00	Jun-21–14 17:31:36 PDT
Charles (4)	US $105.00	Jun-21–14 17:31:32 PDT
Charles (4)	US $100.00	Jun-21–14 17:29:55 PDT
Bob (182 ★)	US $95.00	Jun-19–14 08:50:50 PDT
Alice (1)	US $90.00	Jun-18–14 01:25:14 PDT
Starting price	US $90.00	Jun-17–14 13:12:37 PDT

Note: If two people bid the same amount, the first bid has priority.

engaged in incremental bidding by tendering consecutive bids of $100.00, $105.00, and $113.00. To understand the evolution of the price, the full bid history can be revealed by clicking the link "Show automatic bids." In table 7 is presented the complete history of bids tendered to this point in the auction. The lighter lines, which are new relative to table 6, show bids tendered by eBay's proxy server. In this case Danielle entered a proxy bid of $115.00 on June 18. For the next few days, Charles tried to uncover the minimum bid to overtake Danielle by constantly bidding the minimum amount required above the current high bid

Table 7 Complete bid history for Wayfarers

Bidders: 4 **Bids**: 7 **Time left**: 1 hour 22 mins 51 secs **Duration**: 7 days

Automatic bids may be placed days or hours before a listing ends.

Hide automatic bids

Bidder	Bid amount	Bid time
Charles (4)	**US $117.50**	**Jun-21–14 17:31:42 PDT**
Danielle (87 ★)	US $115.00	Jun-18–14 13:34:39 PDT
Charles (4)	US $113.00	Jun-21–14 17:31:36 PDT
Danielle (87 ★)	US $107.50	Jun-18–14 13:34:39 PDT
Charles (4)	US $105.00	Jun-21–14 17:31:32 PDT
Danielle (87 ★)	US $102.50	Jun-18–14 13:34:39 PDT
Charles (4)	US $100.00	Jun-21–14 17:29:55 PDT
Danielle (87 ★)	US $96.00	Jun-18–14 13:34:39 PDT
Bob (182 ★)	US $95.00	Jun-19–14 08:50:50 PDT
Danielle (87 ★)	US $91.00	Jun-18–14 13:34:39 PDT
Alice (1)	US $90.00	Jun-18–14 01:25:14 PDT
Alice (1)	US $90.00	Jun-18–14 01:25:14 PDT
Starting price	US $90.00	Jun-17–14 13:12:37 PDT

Note: Gray text indicates an automatic (proxy bid) placed by eBay on behalf of the bidder. If two people bid the same amount, the first bid has priority.

(determined by the bid increment above Charles' previous bid since Danielle's proxy bid exceeded this value).

The top three rows are most interesting. When Charles tendered $113.00, eBay's server could not increase the bid by the increment $2.50 because Danielle told the proxy server that she would pay at most $115.00. Thus the proxy server set the current bid at $115.00; were the auction to end now, the first-price rule would apply. Charles finally overtook Danielle with a bid of $117.50—the $115.00 current bid plus the bid increment.

Sniping can be effective when you face an opponent like Charles who does not employ proxy bidding but, for whatever reason, tries to monitor the auction and to respond by bidding the minimum amount above the current high bid. Today buyers can receive text notifications concerning their status at an auction and respond by bidding from their smartphones, so this incremental strategy may become more prevalent than it previously was.

Another reason to snipe is anonymity: late bidding limits the information that rivals have about you. Note that the bidding histories shown in tables 6 and 7 permit you to investigate rivals. Although eBay protects the usernames of bidders, the site still permits rivals to see how often rivals participate at auctions. The numerical values in parentheses after the usernames represent the feedback score an eBayer has achieved (we will discuss this further in the section Reputation). Because positive ratings are more common than negative ones, it is likely correlated with the buyer's experience in bidding.

Some objects at auction may have important common-value components. If resale is possible and bidders differ in their ability to judge the quality of an object (for example, with antiques where some bidders might be experts who frequently bid and others are less informed), then bidding late limits the potential for the less-informed bidders to learn from the experts' private information.

Although these might be considered strategic reasons to justify sniping, other bidders might simply procrastinate or feel uncomfortable about having bids tendered which require them to wait before knowing if it was accepted. In fact eBay provides users the option to display search results that are sorted by the time in which they end, which may be why "late" bids are received.

With the potential benefits of sniping in mind, it is important to note that sniping involves risks as well. By definition, sniping leaves the bidder little time to respond should a tendered bid be insufficient to overtake the current high bid. Snipers also run the risk that late bids may not be successfully transmitted because of traffic jams on the Internet, often referred to as *latencies*. Nonetheless, sniping continues to be a popular approach to Internet auctions. Revisiting our Ray-Ban sunglasses auction, in table 8 we show the final bid history. Six new lines have been added relative to table 7 that represented the situation at the auction with just over an hour left. Alice re-engaged in the auction twice, first overtaking Charles. Danielle then tried one more proxy bid of $151.99, which was ultimately the successful winning bid. Sniping attempts were relevant in this auction—Alice tried to take the object by bidding just four seconds before the auction closed, but Danielle

Table 8 Final auction results for Wayfarers

Bidders: 4 **Bids**: 10 **Time ended**: Jun-24–14 13:12:37 PDT **Duration**: 7 days

Automatic bids may be placed days or hours before a listing ends

Hide automatic bids

Bidder	Bid amount	Bid time
Danielle (87 ★)	**US $151.99**	**Jun-24–14 13:10:32 PDT**
Alice (1)	US $150.50	Jun-24–14 13:12:33 PDT
Danielle (87 ★)	US $130.50	Jun-24–14 13:10:32 PDT
Charles (4)	US $128.00	Jun-21–14 17:31:42 PDT
Charles (4)	US $122.50	Jun-21–14 17:31:42 PDT
Alice (1)	US $120.00	Jun-24–14 13:07:01 PDT
Charles (4)	US $117.50	Jun-21–14 17:31:42 PDT
Danielle (87 ★)	US $115.00	Jun-18–14 13:34:39 PDT
Charles (4)	US $113.00	Jun-21–14 17:31:36 PDT
Danielle (87 ★)	US $107.50	Jun-18–14 13:34:39 PDT
Charles (4)	US $105.00	Jun-21–14 17:31:32 PDT
Danielle (87 ★)	US $102.50	Jun-18–14 13:34:39 PDT
Charles (4)	US $100.00	Jun-21–14 17:29:55 PDT
Danielle (87 ★)	US $96.00	Jun-18–14 13:34:39 PDT
Bob (183 ★)	US $95.00	Jun-19–14 08:50:50 PDT
Danielle (87 ★)	US $91.00	Jun-18–14 13:34:39 PDT
Alice (1)	US $90.00	Jun-18–14 01:25:14 PDT
Alice (1)	US $90.00	Jun-18–14 01:25:14 PDT
Starting price	US $90.00	Jun-17–14 13:12:37 PDT

Note: Gray text indicates an automatic (proxy bid) placed by eBay on behalf of the bidder. If two people bid the same amount, the first bid has priority.

received the item because her proxy bid, tendered about two minutes before the auction closed, was higher. Note, too, that the auction ended under the first-price rule because the winning bid and the second-highest bid were $1.49 apart, while the relevant bid increment in this price range is $2.50.

Sellers are understandably concerned about sniping. Late bids might not be transmitted; even if they are not winning bids, the prices sellers receive will be understated when these tenders do not add competition to the auction. Ways to prevent sniping exist that may favor sellers. An online auction can be designed to have a soft close: the end time is automatically extended for a certain time period when a bid is submitted within a specific interval before the close of the auction. By extending the auction, other bidders have time to respond, thus removing the incentives to snipe. The New Zealand auction site Trade Me uses an automatic extension, prolonging the closing time when any bid is registered in the final two minutes of an auction; auctions will only end when no bids have been received for at least two minutes.

Alternatively, the auction can end at a random time over some interval that cannot be influenced by either the buyers or the seller. Candle auctions were used as early as the fourteenth century to sell ships in England and chattels in France. At these auctions, bidding was only permitted while the flame was lit. When an auction can terminate suddenly, bidders have the incentive to submit serious bids early in the auction. Such auctions allow rivals to respond (provided the candle still burns), unlike at sealed-bid auctions. Still, the outcomes at candle auctions may have some of the properties of the canonical English auction meaning that when common-value components exist, the open format can be important in allowing bids to be observed.

Proxy bidding can be viewed as an attempt to thwart sniping: manually tendered bids can be plagued by latencies, while those tendered by the server are virtually instantaneous. In the Ray-Ban auction, a proxy bid protected bidders from sniping by ensuring that the winning bid was in contention regardless of how late competing bids trickled in. This is typically understood by veteran bidders: both Bob and Danielle had far higher feedback scores and took the proxy system more seriously than Alice and Charles, who both used incremental bidding throughout the auction.

Shill Bidding

Above, we have emphasized the importance of competition in garnering the highest possible price for the seller. Consequently a seller has an incentive to create the illusion of competition. In our discussion of procurement contracts, we noted that the seller might be concerned about collusive activities among the bidders. Another, often illegal (or at least explicitly forbidden) activity is referred to as *shill bidding*. Shill bidding occurs when a confederate of the seller bids at an auction with the sole purpose of driving up the winning price. The shill bidder could be the seller operating under a fictitious name using a different bidder identity or a member of the seller's family or a friend of the seller or an employee of the auctioneer. Shill bids are artificial in the sense that the bidder has no interest in actually winning the item. Shill bidding is a concern to buyers; consumer-protection and antitrust agencies have argued that shill bidding defrauds consumers and challenges the integrity of online auctions.

Concern by buyers over seller (or auctioneer) behavior is not new. At traditional auctions, such shady practice has been known to happen as well. For example, auctioneers at English auctions have been known to employ *chandelier* or *rafter bidding*, sometimes referred to as *taking bids off the wall*; that is, the auctioneer pretends to spot bids in the room either early in the auction or to keep momentum going once the auction is underway. Often the practice is legal, provided it takes place before the reserve price has been met.

Shill bidding can take place at these English auctions as well: some bidders might agree with a seller to buy an object ahead of time at a set price. In exchange, these shill bidders receive a portion of any auction price that exceeds that amount. Thus the accomplice has incentive to bid the object up just to receive a larger profit from the item's sale. Even if the shill bidder wins the auction at a price higher than the preauction agreement, that buyer still gets a discount.

Fake bids can make other buyers falsely feel that more interest exists in the object than is actually the case, perhaps unethically driving up the price earned by the seller. Because auction houses (including Christie's and Sotheby's as well as eBay) generate most of their revenues from commission fees, which are fractions of selling prices, they too have incentive to generate the highest price possible for the seller. Shill bidding can be a concern when employees (real or virtual) engage in such behavior. Although eBay explicitly states that shill bidding is forbidden, the firm clearly benefits from the practice: whether the good is awarded to a truly interested buyer or to an accomplice of the seller, eBay receives a higher commission when shill bids determine the sale price.

Some economists have proposed strategies that allow the seller to shill bid, without becoming the high bidder, provided bidding is sufficiently predictable. For example, bidders might regularly tender amounts that are on the dollar. Interestingly, eBay's pricing rule accommodates such behavior, as one way a seller can have success in shill bidding is through incremental bidding. Remember, incremental bidding may occur because bidders think that the eBay auction is like an English auction and may not realize that proxy bidding is available to them, but it can also help the seller shill bid to drive up price. A shill bidder can continually raise the price by incrementally bidding dollar amounts (if bidders typically bid on the dollar). When the asking price increases by the minimum bid increment, the highest sincere proxy bid is at least as high as the previous price plus the bid increment. If the asking price increases by less, then the highest genuine proxy bid has been discovered.

For example, revisiting the Ray-Ban auction bid history in table 8, Danielle won the auction and used the proxy system twice. Each time her proxy bid was "discovered" as can be seen by how the price evolved. The price change from $113.00 to $115.00 meant the price went up by less than the bid increment so Danielle's proxy bid was revealed. Likewise the winning price involved a difference between the high bid and the previous high bid of less than $2.50, the minimum bid increment, meaning the first-price rule was in effect. Note, too, that both proxies were discovered by bidders with low feedback scores (Charles and Alice), something that would also likely suggest a shill bidder as the accounts may have been created for the sole purpose of deliberately increasing auction prices. Since Charles uncovered Danielle's first proxy bid and then continued to bid, it is unlikely that Charles was a shill bidder. The same is likely true of Alice who bid at multiple points in the auction. A shill bidder might employ this incremental approach and then stop participating as soon as the highest proxy bid is detected. Note that driving this revelation is the presence of the minimum bid increment—the nonstandard way in which the standing price changes.

One way eBay could thwart shill bidding is to set the current asking price at exactly the second-highest bid. Then no way would exist to discover any proxy bid that had been submitted, making shill bidding a riskier tactic.

Shill bidding clearly involves risk, and not just in the legal sense. A seller who participates using another identity risks having the object bought in—his being the highest bid at the end of the auction. The object is never transferred to a sincere buyer and the seller still owes the auction house commission fees and incurs expenses associated with taking the item to auction.

That said, a seller can use shill bidding to save money and to implement an optimal auction. Recall that reserve prices can be used to increase the revenue a seller expects to receive at an auction. To employ a reserve price on eBay involves a separate fee that ranges from $2.00 to $50.00, depending on the reserve price a seller seeks to establish at the auction. This creates an incentive for sellers to shill bid, not to extract every last cent out of the competing bidders, but to avoid the higher listing fee that comes with formally setting a reserve price, while still increasing the expected sale price. Although this type of behavior may seem innocuous or even commendable, it can still harm buyers by stimulating bids as the phony tenders could be interpreted as genuine interest in the object at auction.

Reputation

Aside from antiques, you probably don't hold the market for used goods in high esteem. You might associate used goods with flea markets, garage sales, or thrift stores. Let's do away with those thoughts and consider for a moment the market for used cars. Automobiles are expensive; purchasing one is intimidating to many consumers. Had you the financial resources to do so, you'd likely buy a new car rather than a used one, even when both have the same expected performance and lifespan, perhaps because of the risk of making a bad decision when purchasing a used car. What goes on underneath the hood is often mysterious to drivers who have little understanding of the parts and their function, let alone their reliability. Indeed we give cars that are discovered to be of poor quality a special name: lemons. In *Cars 2*, the lemons are the cars considered ugly and weak—they are the bad guys in the kids' movie.

Nobel laureate George Akerlof modeled the market for used cars to illustrate how the presence of lemons in a market can prevent owners of good cars from even posting them for sale. At the heart of the issue is an asymmetry of information: the owner of a used car knows more about its true quality than any potential buyer. That is, lemons cannot be detected easily, perhaps because they've been poorly maintained, driven hard, repaired by not-so-honest mechanics, or even tampered with in some unobservable way.

Buyers realize that some used cars are lemons; therefore they may be unwilling to pay more than the value of what they expect an average quality car to be. Sellers of good cars will not want to sell good vehicles at the average price, so the best cars do not enter the preowned market. Consequently the average quality of used cars for sale falls below the average quality of used cars at large; buyers then downgrade their views of the average used car for sale. Of course, this process can generate a downward spiral: owners of cars worthy of prices that exceed this revised price will not put those cars on the used market, leading buyers to reduce their expectations of average used cars on the market even further, and so on. In the end, only the cars of the poorest quality exist in the market.

It's amazing that people (ourselves included) are even willing to engage in what amounts to essentially anonymous online auctions—given the uncertainty about the quality of used items combined with concerns about shill bidding, buyers' abilities to make payment, and fraud, let alone the absence of any personal relationship. Not only do buyers not know the sellers, but they have no way of meeting them, they cannot hold and inspect the object for sale, and, at least in the beginning, little protection existed for buyers when interactions went poorly. eBay is not an online retailer: no goods are delivered. The site is a venue for transactions.

The Better Business Bureau would find it difficult to police individual eBay users. Moreover consumer protection agencies can really only give general advice concerning what to look for when dealing with another person online. The solution, of course, is that a mechanism is needed for sellers to signal credibility and quality to potential buyers, and thus earn their trust. In settings where participants interact perhaps only once, it is particularly important that the seller be able to convey to buyers a reputation as being trustworthy, to make buyers comfortable with tendering bids. Although it is now taken for granted, the solution to this problem is to allow participants to build a reputation. In these situations, ratings of market participants induce them to invest in and to build reputations from previous transactions. Online marketplaces like eBay (and most major players in today's "sharing economy" like Uber, AirBnB, and CouchSurfing) rely on the opinions of those who have had prior experience with another participant to convey to others the quality of a potential transaction.

Reputations are particularly important in auction environments; otherwise, asymmetries in information can lead to prices that are below what a seller should receive, just as in the lemons anecdote. Without reputations, good sellers are indistinguishable from bad ones, so incentives

Reputations are particularly important in auction environments; otherwise, asymmetries in information can lead to prices that are below what a seller should receive.

exist for dishonest bad sellers to claim they are good, suppressing prices good sellers would receive and potentially compromising the ability of the market to function at all. Bidders have the incentive to shade their bids if there is some positive probability that the seller might not ship the good or that the good gets delivered in a condition that might not accord with the buyer's expectation. This should concern honest sellers who now face the prospect of auction prices that are below what someone might pay for the object in a face-to-face transaction.

Feedback scores provide a signal and can reduce the market failure that results from dealing with anonymous buyers and sellers. eBay's feedback system allows each party to a transaction to award positive (+1), neutral (0), or negative (−1) perspective on the interaction. Such scores are aggregated over all transactions and provided publicly. Recall the numbers in parentheses after the list of bidders in the Ray-Ban auction. eBay indicates reputation levels by providing different colored stars that correspond to different numerical ratings. Further details (such as the percentage of positive feedback and categorical ratings concerning the accuracy of object descriptions, communication, shipping time and charges, and detailed feedback) can be learned by clicking on specific eBay users. By allowing buyers and sellers to rate each other and then providing this information to all potential participants, eBay essentially (and cleverly) crowdsources regulation to those who use the website. eBay avoids having to monitor buyers and sellers or to certify items being sold.

Sellers must consider carefully their actions because current buyers can rate their experiences and sellers' reputations are taken seriously by buyers. Consequently sellers face a trade-off when determining how to behave in a given transaction: invest in and maintain a good reputation in the hope of benefiting from good behavior in future transactions or take advantage of the buyer in a current transaction. By being honest, the seller hopes to receive positive feedback from the buyers thereby improving (or at least maintaining) the current reputation. By being deceptive, the seller can earn a higher price in the current transaction, but risks being exposed, which devalues future transactions. Reputation is an asset. Because feedback scores reflecting peer-to-peer ratings serve as the sole indicator of trust and counterparty risk, this begs the question: does a reputation have value?

The seller needs an incentive to behave honestly, to maintain a reputation. Using ungraded baseball cards for which sellers reported the condition of the cards, researchers have found that those with better reputations were more honest. This finding suggests that feedback scores reflect the attributes that are missing from repeated relationships—in a word: trust. Researchers analyzing the determinants of sale prices on eBay have also found, perhaps not surprisingly, that high-reputation sellers receive higher prices: if higher feedback scores mean buyers can trust certain sellers, then those sellers will garner higher prices at auction. Moreover feedback scores seem to matter more for high-priced goods than for low-priced ones, perhaps not just because more is on the line with a high-price sale but also because more thought is put into the purchase and reputation is weighed seriously. Reputation in a self-enforcing market can thus serve as a barrier to entry, generating more income to the experienced, reputable participants.

Reputation is not symmetric: negative ratings often have a much greater downward effect on final auction prices than positive ones have on increasing final auction prices. Negative feedback has also been shown to decrease sales growth for regular sellers; subsequent unfavorable opinions come more rapidly than the initial poor ratings. Obviously participants can create new accounts to avoid repercussions from previous deceitful behavior, a practice that can undermine the potential value of feedback rating systems. Researchers have found that a seller is more likely to exit the market when negative feedback has been received. To make shedding a reputation more difficult, eBay requires that sellers provide not just name and address but also telephone number, an automatic payment method for paying seller fees, and suggests a verified PayPal account (which requires your banking information), thus increasing the concerns that sellers have for positive buyer feedback and also making deceptive and fraudulent behavior more costly. At a minimum, sellers who adopt a new pseudonym must reset their history—start from scratch. Beginning afresh has its own costs—lower auction prices until a good reputation has been established.

Reputation mechanisms have been developed to establish histories for users so that participants in future transactions can form expectations about their interactions. Although repeated relationships might be rare and personal ones nonexistent, the sheer number of independent transactions that take place for individual sellers can be levered to reassure or to warn future buyers. Thus online auction markets can mimic important features of relationships such as trust, and this ensures that such markets are not just over-run by lemons. Reputations in fact are so valuable that they might be a reasonable substitute for warranty policies. For example, eBay often offers product guarantees in the form of "guaranteed or your money back" promises. Indeed, once reputations have been factored in by consumers, some researchers have found such policies are largely ineffective, though others have found warranties complement reputations in generating higher sales prices.

In 2002 eBay acquired PayPal, a company that provides a safe way for money to be exchanged by strangers, increasing the confidence buyers have in dealing with non-established outlets. Although developing reputations and innovations in security have clearly played a role in allowing eBay to become the "World's Online Marketplace," the company adopted a new slogan in 2011 that upset used-good sellers and could detract from its auction business: "Buy it new. Buy it now."

Buy It Now

Although eBay's advertising team didn't brand the slogan until 2011, the opportunity to end an auction early at a prespecified price had been available since November 2000. Specifically, sellers can put objects up for auction along with a posted fixed price, referred to as the *Buy It Now* (BIN) price. Reserve prices ensure minimum revenues for the seller and can increase expected revenues, but what about maximum prices? On eBay, the posted price is available to anyone before a bid has been tendered. Once a bid has been tendered, however, the BIN opportunity disappears, and the sale continues according to the auction format, thereby creating a hybrid of auction and fixed-price mechanisms. Other online auction sites have been known to employ auctions at which the buy price is available throughout the bidding, so it actually can represent a maximum auction price. Although introducing so-called buy prices may seem inconsequential, historically it has made a remarkable difference. Why?

The BIN option can be a way for sellers to receive prices that exceed what they would expect at a standard eBay auction when buyers are risk averse. A risk-averse bidder is willing to pay a higher price to ensure winning the object rather than go through the risk that an auction involves. Consequently posted prices can build in risk premia that are higher the more risk averse are bidders. Augmenting ascending-price auctions with buy prices can even increase expected revenues beyond what a pay-your-bid or Dutch auction would achieve. Similarly sellers can use the fixed prices to garner higher revenue when buyers are impatient. As mentioned, sellers can choose from auction durations of one, three, five, seven, or ten days. If bidders discount the future severely relative to the present, then briefer auctions will be preferred because they will increase bidder participation. Of course, briefer auctions imply that the object could go unsold before interested buyers have a chance to learn about or view the posting, meaning the number of potential bidders would be smaller. The hybrid mechanism allows sellers to exploit the impatience of bidders by building in a time premium that a bidder must pay to avoid the time-consuming bidding process.

Yet sellers could mistakenly underprice the object by setting a buy price that is too low, essentially leaving money on the table. Some bidders may get entertainment or experiential value from participating at the auction. In short, they would be willing to pay a premium to participate, even if it means paying a price that exceeds the buy price. Of course, any benefit that might accrue to the seller from bidder emotions or excitement is forgone when the object is swooped up before the first bid is cast. The arguments from the previous paragraph can also be flipped around if the seller is impatient or risk averse—in which case, lower buy prices allow the object to sell earlier or with less variance.

The innovation of the BIN option and success of massive online retailers like Amazon led to a shift in the composition of activity taking place on eBay. The company's growth was fueled by proxy bidding—buyers no longer needed to monitor auctions constantly, thus allowing them to avoid associated transaction costs. Nevertheless, online consumers seem wedded to the brick-and-mortar tradition of posted prices, so in 2002, eBay began allowing sellers to avoid auction listings all together by listing items with only BIN prices. Today BIN-only listings pool together listings by individual sellers with inventory from retailers such as Toys "R" Us, Home Depot, and Target and dominate auction offerings on eBay. Given the benefits of auctions that we've advocated, this suggests a puzzle: why have we left auctions only to return to posted prices? Were auctions just a segue from offline shopping to a similar format in an online world?

Researchers have suggested the shift to posted prices results from a fundamental change in consumer preferences.

In the early years of the Internet, online auctions were new, exciting, and could serve as a form of entertainment. The journey to obtaining an object and the story that could be told was as exciting as the object itself. Now, however, time spent online has a higher opportunity cost. Social networking sites (like Facebook, Twitter, LinkedIn, and Pinterest) allow users to connect with family and friends or with others sharing similar interests. News-reporting websites, blogs, and Wikipedia allow people to learn about current events, consider different perspectives, or see which actress starred in that movie that came up earlier. And what other movies has she been in? With everything available instantaneously, this mentality might have transferred into our purchasing habits as well. Search engines have improved dramatically, allowing consumers to compare prices online easily to ensure that shoppers are getting a good deal (or at least not overpaying too much). Why wait to see if an object can be acquired at auction, then have the seller personally ship the item, when it takes hardly more than a click on a mobile device to have something express shipped from a warehouse and ready for you in just a couple days. With decreased demand for auctions, sellers using auctions expect lower prices. This shift implies that bidders might get items at auction at bargain prices, but because of the "inconvenience" this price discount can be likened to that of coupons in which price-sensitive consumers need to exert effort to get the reward of a lower price.

Underneath the observation that items can be acquired through alternative outlets is a more fundamental observation: other items exist. Thus far we have focused on the behavior of bidders when a single object is sold. Auctions, especially those online, are not conducted in isolation. For example, searching for "Ray-Ban Wayfarer Sunglasses" on eBay led to 4,521 different listings. With many offerings all happening simultaneously, a richer framework is required to analyze bidder behavior. How should a seller auction off goods when several units exist to sell? Should each be sold sequentially or should they all be sold in one fell swoop? Certainly the formats of the various possible auctions structure incentives in a way that leads bidders to behave differently, so which will be best in different situations? To consider these, let's shift our attention to auctions for multiple units and multiple objects.

MULTI-UNIT AND
MULTI-OBJECT AUCTIONS

Imagine you've just been admitted to MIT's Sloan School of Management. Before you even set foot in a classroom, your first challenge is to win seats in some classes. Like business schools at Virginia, Berkeley, Columbia, and Chicago, the Sloan School uses auctions to determine who gets to attend which courses. Moreover bidding is not just for MBAs: undergraduates at Colorado College must also win the right to attend courses at auctions. Law students at Vanderbilt, Memphis, and Harvard bid to attend courses too.

Under these systems each student is endowed with a fixed number of points that can vary depending on year in the program—for example, an upper-year student may get more than a newly-admitted student. In order to attend a course, a student must then bid some of these points. Those students tendering the highest bids earn seats in the class. In aggregate, however, across all courses, no student can bid more than the number of points allocated: therein lies the trade-off. You can bid all your points for a course you really want to take, but that means you won't have any points remaining, and will be allocated to courses that have excess capacity, often courses only a few think are interesting.

The number of bidding rounds as well as whether bidding is required for core courses, whether points can be transferred across terms or academic years, or if refunds are possible should a student drop a course can vary across schools, but in all cases, bidding at auctions determines course allocations. With students paying great sums in tuition every year, administrators must decide how to deal with resource constraints. Auctions provide a transparent, equitable way of allocating scarce resources. Auctions aren't just used for courses either; MBAs at Dartmouth, Duke, and Northwestern may bid for open slots to interview with recruiters as well.

Auctioning the rights to attend courses is an example of a multi-object auction—each course is different. Conversely, several units of the same object can be sold at auction. For example, in order to borrow money, the US Treasury sells securities (bills, notes, and bonds) every week. The specific financial instruments at auction are, for instance, five-year notes or 26-week bills. These financial instruments are sold in increments of $100 to commercial banks, foreign governments, and world investors. Which

$100 increment any investor wins is really irrelevant; they are all the same.

Higher tenders mean bidders are willing to pay the government more now for the right to receive $100 when the financial instrument matures. In short, these high prices translate into low interest rates. When borrowing, the US government prefers lower interest rates to higher ones. Consequently the government prefers high prices because they imply low interest rates: the winners of the auction are the highest bidders, those willing to accept the lowest discounts.

US Treasury auctions are important for at least two reasons: first, trillions of dollars are raised every year; second, the discount rates determined at these auctions reflect how investors feel about the health of the American economy. Although the US government has never defaulted on its debt, the outcomes of the auctions gauge sentiments concerning the nation's economic growth prospects.

In short, multi-object auctions involve the sale of several different objects, whereas multi-unit auctions involve the sale of several units of the same object. Obviously the objects and the units can be either packaged together or sold individually. In either case the most basic question faced by the seller is whether to sell everything at the same time (a simultaneous auction) or consecutively (a sequential auction).

In short, multi-object auctions involve the sale of several different objects, while multi-unit auctions involve the sale of several units of the same object.

In the United States, when allocating bands of electromagnetic spectrum for wireless use, the Federal Communications Commission conducts simultaneous, multiple-round auctions. The licenses involve the right to transmit signals over specific, related bands of the spectrum in different regions. Although multiple licenses sometimes exist in a given market, this is a multi-object auction—Los Angeles is different from Seattle. Within this setting, participants may bid on any collection of licenses during a given round. At the end of the round, if any licenses received bids, the prices for those objects are increased. Bidders then learn which rights they currently stand to win and which they may have been outbid by rivals. Having processed this information, the next round of bidding proceeds where bidders can again proffer tender on any of the licenses. The auction ends when, in a given round, no bidder challenges or tenders a higher offer for *any* of the licenses at auction.

In contrast, consider an auction of a case of twelve bottles of a specific vintage of wine. At Sotheby's Finest and Rarest Wines, on June 21, 2014, in New York, the third lot (object) to hit the block was a case of Château Haut Brion 1990. After that sold for $9,188, lots four through eight were also cases of Château Haut Brion 1990. Following the sequential sale of the 1990 vintage, lots nine through eleven each contained cases of Château Haut Brion 1995. This sale is referred to as a *sequential, multi-unit auction* because each unit (lot, case of wine) is auctioned individually. After the hammer falls, another unit is sold, and so on. Wine auctions are in fact quite interesting because winning a lot often entitles the winning bidder to invoke the "buyer's option." In short, under the buyer's option, the winner has the right to purchase any or all of the remaining lots at the current, winning price. Why do this? If sequential auctions take a long time to conduct, then the buyer's option can speed-up the sale. The buyer's option has also been observed at fish, flower, and fur auctions (to name just three). Thus, although the sale is structured as one in which separate auctions are conducted one at a time, rules sometimes exist that link units for sale.

Multi-object and multi-unit auctions play an important role in the world's economic system. Each year, permits allowing sulfur dioxide emission are sold at auction by the Environmental Protection Agency to utilities and brokers as well as environmental groups. In Virginia, permits to emit nitrogen oxides are sold at auction. The Regional Greenhouse Gas Initiative auctions carbon dioxide allowances every quarter. Auctions are at the forefront of the European Union's Emission Trading System and will likely play a role in regulating greenhouse gas emissions in the United States.

Auctions are also used by national and state governments to procure electricity. Power-grid operators construct forecasts of electricity demand in future years and auction the right to provide this energy on a certain delivery date. These auctions are important not just because they concern billions of dollars, but also because they dictate the types of investments (renewable energy, efficiency improvements, fossil fuels) made today. Moreover auctions have been proposed as solutions to such national problems as deficit spending and corporate taxation as well as ways for small businesses and start-up companies to raise money through crowdfunding.

The director of the Temporary Migration Cluster, Giovanni Peri (an economist at the University of California, Davis), suggested on National Public Radio's *Planet Money* podcast that work-based visas should be sold at auction: by awarding US immigration slots to the highest bidders, auctions would ensure firms that benefit the most would be able to hire foreign workers.

Having highlighted some examples of multi-object and multi-unit auctions, let's examine commonly used pricing rules. To avoid complications and confusion, in describing the mechanisms, we focus on the case where several units of the same object are sold at auction. Nevertheless, much of this discussion extends to the case when several different objects are sold and we investigate such a setting in chapter 8. Rather than characterize bidder behavior fully, however, we simply note some interesting implications that different pricing rules have on the incentives of bidders; in the next chapter, we consider a specific market in more detail.

Types of Multi-Unit Auctions

Multi-unit auctions can involve either open or sealed-bid formats, but because other considerations can be important when several objects or units are sold, a richer set of pricing rules are employed at such auctions. To see how other factors can play a role in the pricing rules, first consider what bids look like in these settings. Suppose that Alice and Bob are vying for three units of a homogeneous good sold at a sealed-bid auction (for example, three cases of identical wine). Each will tender a list of bids indicating a willingness to pay for each additional unit won. For example, suppose that Alice submits the list ($12, $11, $8) and Bob tenders the list ($9, $4, $0). In this case Bob does not want more than two units of the good: the third bid in his list is zero. At standard multi-unit auctions, the bids are ordered from highest to lowest and the units for sale are allocated to the respective high bidders. In this case Alice wins two units and Bob one. Fortunately, the auction formats and pricing rules used when several objects are for sale correspond with the auctions we've investigated thus far in the book.

The pay-your-bid pricing rule is extended so that a bidder pays the sum of winning bids. In the example above, Alice wins two units and pays $12 + $11 = $23, and Bob wins one unit and pays $9. In introductory microeconomics courses, students first encounter situations in which firms charge consumers different prices for the same good—a practice referred to as *price discrimination*. Since bidders typically obtain the units for different prices, pay-your-bid auctions are commonly referred to as *discriminatory auctions*.

Alternatively, recall that at second-price, sealed-bid auctions the price paid by the winner is determined by the second-highest bid. In multi-unit settings, a unique market-clearing price is typically set by the highest losing bid. In the example with Alice and Bob, the highest losing bid is set by Alice, $8. Thus Alice wins two units, at $8 each, and must pay $16, whereas Bob wins one unit at $8. Because all bidders pay the same price, these are referred to as *uniform-price* auctions. In this example, revenues earned under the uniform-pricing rule are lower than under the pay-your-bid rule, but that is because we have maintained the same bid lists across the pricing rules. In reality, we know that bidders' equilibrium behavior will differ depending on the pricing rule used.

Given our understanding of single-object auctions, the above two pricing rules are the most natural, but the only thing limiting the use of other pricing rules is a designer's imagination. For example, consider the multi-unit extension of the Vickrey auction which we refer to as the *generalized Vickrey auction* (GVA) as it simplifies to a Vickrey auction if one object is at auction. Again, bidders submit sealed tenders, but at a GVA, prices differ across units sold (as in the discriminatory auction) and are determined by nonwinning bids (as in uniform-price auctions). Under the GVA pricing rule, when a bidder submits an amount that exceeds that of other bidders, those who have been outbid are in some sense hurt; economists refer to this implicit cost (which involves no actual payment or monetary transfer to the bidder who has been outbid) as an *externality*. Rivals who experience this externality, by no longer winning units, are the ones who set the price paid by the winning bidders.

In the example, were Alice not at the auction, Bob would have won all three units. Given Bob was willing to pay $4 and $0 for the second and third units, respectively, when Alice participates in the auction and wins, she should only pay those prices for her two units; thus she pays $4 total. Likewise, were Bob not at the auction, Alice would have won all three units rather than just two. Alice would have paid $8 for the third unit, so Bob should pay $8 for the one unit he won. The pricing rule can be extended to admit more players as well as other types of bidding—for example, bidding for bundles of objects.

Suppose now that Charles participates and submits the list ($7, $3, $2). In this case the units would still be allocated to Alice (two units) and Bob (one unit), but Charles' presence and behavior is important in determining the prices they pay. Were Alice absent from the auction, Bob would have won two units and Charles one unit. Thus Alice, who offered to pay $23 for these two units, should pay the opportunity cost of her winning, which is $11. When Alice takes home the units, she generates an externality— the next-best use for these units would have provided a benefit of $7 to Charles and $4 to Bob; Bob still pays $8 given Alice would have won the unit he takes home if Bob were absent, even if Charles participated.

Like these sealed-bid extensions, open formats exist in multi-unit settings as well. For example, a multi-unit Dutch auction involves the auctioneer lowering prices until a bidder is willing to pay the current asking price. The bidder is then awarded a unit and the price continues to drop, again until a bidder indicates a willingness to pay the going price. This process continues until all units are sold. It may seem that the outcomes at these Dutch auctions will be consistent with those at discriminatory auctions. Indeed, given valuations are private, behavior at multi-unit Dutch auctions will be the same as that in a discriminatory setting. However, the strong form of strategic equivalence that existed in single-object settings no longer holds when bidder valuations are interdependent. In the single-object setting, no chance existed for information to be revealed because, as soon as a bidder was awarded the object, the auction ended. With several units, however, the prices at which prior units are sold can be used by other bidders to revise their own valuations.

At multi-unit English auctions, bidders indicate how many units they are willing to purchase at the current asking price. Such reports are aggregated across all bidders: if the revealed demand exceeds the supply at auction, then the price is increased. As the price rises, bidders naturally reduce the number of units they are willing to purchase. The auction ends at a proposed price where the quantity demanded equals the number of units at auction. All units are sold to the interested buyers at that common price. Thus the multi-unit English auction achieves the same outcome as its sealed-bid sister, the uniform-price auction, provided bidders have private values. Any dependence among the valuations of bidders will upset this result. Information is revealed at oral, ascending-price auctions, but not under the sealed-bid format: the two are no longer strategically equivalent. Of course, this is less surprising than the multi-unit, Dutch-discriminatory relationship as the lack of equivalence existed in the single-object setting as well.

Another auction, which is the open version of the GVA, is referred to as *Ausubel auction*, in honor of its inventor Lawrence Ausubel who proposed, developed, investigated, and eventually patented the mechanism. The Ausubel auction was designed with two goals in mind: first, to divorce the prices paid from the bids made; second, to allow information to be released through dynamic prices. Operationally, the Ausubel auction has much in common with the English auction: bidders report how many units they are interested in acquiring at the proposed price. Recall that at GVAs, prices reflect the opportunity cost of each unit going to its winning bidder. At an Ausubel auction, an auctioneer tallies not just the aggregate number of units demanded at each price but also the number of units that would be demanded were each bidder removed from the participant pool. We refer to this latter amount as the *rivals' demand*. It is the difference between the total demand at a given price and a bidder's own demand, accounting for the number of units that a given bidder's rivals would like to purchase at that price. As the auctioneer raises the price, the aggregated quantities corresponding to the total demand and rivals' demand eventually fall.

Imagine Alice is the first bidder for which her rivals' demand is less than the number of units at auction. This means Alice will have secured at least one item. At an Ausubel auction the pricing rule dictates that, for that unit, she should be charged the current price which is responsible for Alice's rivals' demand falling below the available quantity. Now the number of remaining units will be the number of units initially for sale, minus the one that Alice will receive and her demand decreases by one unit. The auctioneer continues to augment the price and compare the rivals' demands of the bidders to the number of remaining units. Each time the rivals' demand associated with a given bidder falls below the number of remaining units, an item is awarded to that bidder at the price that instigated such a change and that bidder's demand is reduced by one unit. In this manner the amount charged to each winning bidder reflects the willingness to pay of the bidder who would have won the unit, had the winning bidder not participated in the auction. Like the equivalence between the multi-unit English and the uniform-price auction as well as the multi-unit Dutch and discriminatory auction, the Ausubel auction yields the same outcome as a GVA, provided bidders have independent private valuations.

Hybrid pricing rules in multi-object and multi-unit settings can be employed as well. Consider a 200-level ticket to a Northwestern University men's basketball game. Northwestern (thanks to the advice of two economists on staff) uses something referred to as *Purple Pricing*. Essentially the university employs a Dutch auction to award seats: the price for a seat starts high and then falls as game day approaches. Fans can buy tickets at any point until all seats are gone. You might be concerned about fairness: doesn't this mean that fans buying tickets earlier end up paying higher prices? If budget-constrained fanatics wait too long when trying to obtain lower prices, then might they underestimate demand and end up trying to scalp a ticket on game day? Actually Purple Pricing addresses both of these concerns through its pricing rule with something referred to as the *Purple Pledge*: all fans in a given seat category pay the same price for their tickets. Of course, this means all fans will pay the price paid by the fan getting the ticket for the cheapest price—the fan who waited the longest.

Northwestern refunds early buyers who paid higher prices the difference between what they paid and the lowest price at which a ticket sold. Thus the university uses a uniform-price, Dutch auction to sell category-specific tickets—in other words, a multi-unit auction.

Properties of Multi-Unit Auctions

At multi-unit auctions each bidder receives a valuation for each unit on sale. As before, these valuations are modeled as random draws from an urn. At this point it is natural to sort the valuations from largest to smallest because then each successive valuation can be interpreted as the additional benefit a bidder would obtain from acquiring another unit, given the number of units the bidder currently has. Suppose that the valuations are drawn independently from the same urn. Thus the symmetric IPV model applies and the equivalence relationships between the discriminatory and multi-unit Dutch, the uniform-price and the multi-unit English, and the GVA and the Ausubel auctions hold. In what follows, we focus on their sealed-bid counterparts.

When analyzing bidder behavior, the GVA is a natural starting point because it is the extension of the second-price, sealed-bid auction from our single-object setting. Why? Recall that at single-object Vickrey auctions bidders have a weakly dominant strategy to bid their valuations.

The same is true of bidders at a GVA. In the single-object case the price paid by the winning bidder is unaffected by the winner's behavior because the price is determined by the second-highest bid. By construction, the GVA pricing rule extends this property to a multi-unit setting by ensuring that the price paid by each winner, on every unit, is solely determined by the amount of a rival competing bid. This means a bidder can do no better by under- or overreporting his willingness to pay for any unit. At best, a deviation from truth-telling yields the same outcome for a bidder. For any deviation from honesty, however, a situation exists where the bidder either overpays for additional units or fails to win units that the bidder would have been willing to purchase when the auction concludes. Thus the bid list that reveals a bidder's true valuations remains optimal. Consequently the GVA achieves an efficient allocation because the units are awarded to the participants tendering the highest bids.

Debates weighing efficiency versus equity arise regularly in nearly all economic problems; the GVA is a good example that illustrates this tension at auctions. One can easily argue that the GVA, while efficient, is unfair. In the example with Alice and Bob, Alice valued each unit more than Bob, yet she pays nothing for one unit and gets the other for $4. In contrast, Bob values each unit less than Alice, but pays $8 for the one unit he wins—twice what Alice paid for both units she takes home.

In claiming that the GVA is the natural generalization of the (single-object) second-price, sealed-bid auction, we are implicitly suggesting that the uniform-price auction is not, despite some compelling similarities to the second-price, sealed-bid auction. Recall that the price paid for all units in the uniform-price auction is the highest losing bid, which means this bid may in fact belong to one of the winning bidders—something that could not happen in the GVA setting where prices paid by winning bidders were always determined by the bids of rivals. Like the GVA, it is a weakly dominant strategy for bidders at uniform-price auctions to bid their valuation for the first unit for the same reasons we suggested in the single-object Vickrey auction as bidders can be assured that if they win just one unit, their bid for that unit will not determine the price paid. At uniform-price auctions, however, bidders do have an incentive to shade their bids on the additional units they demand. Submitting a bid list can be thought of as reporting a demand schedule that indicates the number of units a bidder would purchase at every possible price. Thus bid shading corresponds to a bidder suggesting lower quantities that he would be willing to purchase at some prices. Economists refer to this behavior as *demand reduction*.

In formulating a bid on additional units, a bidder must recognize that higher bids increase the chance other units are won, but because there is also potential for one of the bidder's own tenders on a unit to determine the market-clearing price, an incentive exists to tender lower bids. Note that the potential price-setting effect would apply to all units a bidder wins given the single-price rule, so the incentive to demand-reduce increases with the number of units available. Unless examples are highly stylized, bidding strategies cannot be explicitly solved for at these auctions. Nevertheless, in equilibrium, bidders shade their bids by different amounts depending on their valuation for each unit and, importantly, how many units they have won. Because the number of units won differs across participants, this generates asymmetric behavior (differential shading) across bidders vying to acquire their next unit. As we know from our relaxing the assumption of the symmetric IPV model in the single-object setting, asymmetric behavior means inefficient allocations can arise. Thus, when bidders demand multiple units, because of demand reduction, the uniform-price auction need not be efficient, making it less like the single-object, second-price auctions. Although the uniform-price auction may not be efficient, it appears fair because all winning bidders end up paying the same amount for each unit. Moreover the uniform-price auction provides a clear method of price discovery by determining a unique, market-clearing price.

At discriminatory auctions, bidders will also strategically reduce demand because under this format the payments winning bidders make are determined entirely by their behavior. Thus, in equilibrium, participants will shade their bids for each unit (including the first) in order to guarantee positive payoffs should they win. Behavior at these auctions is complex because each bidder values each unit differently.

As such, Alice may be bidding for her first unit but competing with Bob who is bidding for his second unit. The urn of first-unit valuations is different from the urn of second-unit valuations. Recall figure 5, which depicted bidding strategies for two bidders at an asymmetric first-price auction. The figure illustrated a phenomenon that the weaker bidder behaves more aggressively than the stronger bidder. In the multi-unit setting, a bidder's highest valuation is assigned to the first unit they bid on, while the second-highest valuation corresponds with the second unit. Like our strong-versus-weak bidder example, those bidders trying to acquire their first unit can be considered strong and those vying for later units are weaker. As we know from figure 5 (and the discussion based on it), weaker bidders should behave relatively more aggressively. In the multi-unit setting, however, bid lists should be nonincreasing. To reconcile these different prescriptions, it is quite possible that bidders with valuations for consecutive units that are sufficiently close submit bid lists with constant bids. Similarly, if valuations are far enough apart, then bids for later units will be lower than bids for earlier units. Because behavior is asymmetric across units, the discriminatory auction can be inefficient when bidders demand multiple units, or when each demands just one unit but valuations are drawn from different distributions; behavior in the multi-unit setting is less aggressive the more units that are available for a given level of competition. Whether it is fair is likely a subjective issue—winning bidders pay different amounts for the units they win, but these payments are amounts they willingly revealed during the auction.

Expected Revenue and Practical Considerations

Determining which auction format and pricing rule to use in a given setting is a difficult task. Even large government agencies continue to wrestle with this question; for example, in 1992 the US Treasury switched from a discriminatory to a uniform-price rule (as the economics Nobel laureate Milton Friedman had proposed in the 1960s). In 2001, under the New Electricity Trading Arrangements, the United Kingdom went the other way in conducting its electricity auctions by electing to use a discriminatory format instead of the previous uniform-price format. During the California electricity crisis, the California Power Exchange considered switching to a discriminatory format, but opted against it. Making these choices requires specific empirical knowledge concerning bidders' demand.

Although some auctions, such as the FCC's spectrum auction have specific goals (such as efficiency and allocation to small or underrepresented types of firms, like the bid preference policies discussed earlier), revenue considerations are almost always important to the seller. For example, the US Treasury would like to sell debt at the lowest cost possible. Thus far we have been silent as to the revenue ranking of the multi-unit auction formats which begs the obvious: what can be said about expected revenues in these settings?

Recall that the revenue equivalence theorem prevailed in our single-object benchmark model, but that required the auction to be efficient, something we have found difficult to guarantee in our multi-unit auction formats. If the probability each bidder wins each unit he demands given equilibrium bidding behavior is the same across auction formats, then the revenue equivalence theorem holds. An example of this would be when bidders are symmetric and each demands just one unit, but many units are up for sale. The intuition for this is based on the single-object result along with the recognition that all the formats we have discussed are efficient, meaning their assignment rule is the same, in this setting. In general, however, we know the GVA is efficient, but the discriminatory and uniform-price auctions are not, meaning the assignment of the units differs across formats and the revenue equivalence theorem breaks down. Unfortunately, economists also know that no general revenue ranking exists. That is, examples can be constructed that yield different preferences for the formats in terms of revenue.

Although the lack of a general ranking is in some sense unfortunate, it is also reasonably good news for economists—demand for advice concerning auction design will continue. Specifically, policy advice can be based on a strong understanding of the setting before the auction is put in place, as the formats can be ranked in particular settings. Understanding special features of a market is imperative; prescriptions are case-specific. For example, if it is reasonable to assume that bidders' valuations are constant across units and are generated from a common process (so bidders value all units in the same way, but this differs across bidders), then the seller will maximize revenues by ensuring an efficient allocation—that is, the GVA should be employed. Moreover, because bidders in this example will shade their bids on each unit by equal amounts in a discriminatory setting, the discriminatory auction will generate higher expected revenues than the uniform-price auction.

How comfortable bidders are with auction rules determines the performance of real-world auctions. If the pricing rule or auction dynamics are too complicated, then entry into the market may be reduced, which will dilute the competitive environment, perhaps the most critical factor in determining revenues in any setting. For example, the uniform-price auction may be preferred because of its simple, transparent (and perhaps fair) pricing rule. US Treasury auctions that were converted to the uniform-price rule saw broader participation. In contrast, the discriminatory auction might be a way to extract high prices from bidders, and bidders typically understand that they will be responsible for the amounts they tender on the various units. Although the GVA is efficient, the pricing rule is quite complicated, which could reduce bidder participation.

Of course, the potential challenges we have noted at the single-object auctions remain at multi-unit auctions: valuations may be interdependent, asymmetries may exist, certain mechanisms are more vulnerable to collusion than others, and so on. These further compound the complexity of the auction design and bid formulation. If bidder collusion is a valid concern, then the auctioneer should perhaps consider a sealed-bid rather than an open format. Under the sealed-bid format, less opportunity exists for bidders to communicate, especially if the participants interact in such settings infrequently; under an open format, bidders may develop clever ways to communicate or retaliate within the auction—recall that this happened in the early FCC spectrum auctions. When valuations are dependent and considerable uncertainty exists concerning objects' true values, the open format will reassure bidders as the auction progresses and allow for improved price discovery. Of course, time requirements can vary across formats. Sealed-bid formats are simple to conduct and bidders need only prepare tenders once; open formats, especially in multi-unit settings, can be long, imposing an implicit cost on all participants. Although seemingly a minor issue, the open-format German 3G spectrum auction of August 2000, which lasted for 14 days and the open-format Indian 3G spectrum of 2010, which lasted for 34 days, illustrate the point.

Even though a large variety of auction formats, pricing rules, bidder behavior, and properties of multi-unit auctions have been described in this chapter, we acknowledge fully that many other interesting questions related to these settings exist. For example, should all units be sold at once or in separate auctions that might be held sequentially? The relationship between multiple distinct objects could be important—whether the different objects are viewed as substitute goods or as complementary ones by the bidders. Might it be best for the seller to bundle some of the objects at auction? Rather than continue a general discussion of these issues, we use what we have presented as a starting point to delve into a specific context. In the next chapter we examine online advertising, which allows us to uncover the intricacies of a setting that is both economically important and, as we have found, somewhat mysterious to many.

ONLINE AD AUCTIONS

In April 2014 Google revealed an incredible statistic: 100 billion Google searches per month—on average, over 38 thousand each second. No surprise then that Google is one the most valuable companies in the world. But how does the company convert those billions of searches into revenues? Surprise, surprise—using auctions.

Auctions have been part of Google since its corporate birth. When the company went public on August 19, 2004, it eschewed the traditional "book-building" approach, which involves underwriters who solicit investors to generate demand, and opted instead to sell its shares at what Wall Street dubbed a "multi-unit Dutch auction." Interested investors submitted bids in the form of price-quantity pairs. At each price the quantities demanded by investors were aggregated. The shares of the initial public offering were then sold at the highest price for which the number of shares demanded equaled the number of shares offered. All shares were sold at this market-clearing price, with those investors willing to pay more than this price winning the quantities they requested. In the last chapter we referred to this as a uniform-price auction.

Although many Internet searchers perceive Google as a free public service, the company generates revenues through advertising—Google's most important use of auctions. In 2013 Google earned over $50 billion in revenues from various advertising channels. Auctions are conducted nearly every time you search for some phrase using the Google search engine. Google provides potential advertisers with the opportunity to attract customers by posting formatted copy at the top or alongside Google search results. Economists refer to these as *sponsored search* or *position* auctions.

Auctions are used even when you visit a regular website. You need not use Google (or other search engines like Bing or Yahoo!, which use a similar structure for sponsored search) to run an auction or to generate money for one of these websites: advertisements on regular websites are awarded using auctions as well. Economists refer to these as *display advertising* auctions.

Sponsored Search Auctions

Querying different terms in a search engine yields not only different results, but also different paid ads. The famous department store merchant John Wanamaker once said

Half the money I spend on advertising is wasted; the trouble is I don't know which half.

To reduce the waste, companies target their ads: they are willing to pay more for relevant opportunities than for irrelevant ones.

Consider searching for "diapers"; Google will return thousands of hits, some organic, others are ads. Google marks the ads by placing small boxes with the word "Ad" or "Ads" in the portions of the returned page that does not involve organic search results. A thin horizontal bar also separates ads from the actual search results. Advertisers submit bids to Google for searches involving keywords believed relevant to their ads, with the positions of ads on the page depending on the relative value (score) of various keywords. Google then awards the ad positions (hence the alternative name "position auctions") to the interested parties through an auction. Thus, before your search results are returned to you, an auction has already been held.

This was not always the case. Initially online advertising was conducted the old-fashioned way—through back-and-forth negotiations and via direct sales to advertising firms, which generated inefficiencies for all parties involved. Moreover, in the words of Internet firms: "It's not scalable." You can't expand the activity to literally millions of keyword combinations without hiring tens of thousands of humans, who are costly to employ. Thus Google and other Internet firms needed an approach that could be scaled, algorithmically on a computer.

Under the auction format used, for each search, the right to a consumer's attention is awarded to the firms willing to pay the most for the opportunity. Although several advertising opportunities exist on a given page of search results, not all such opportunities are created equal: positions at the top of the page are more likely to be chosen than those shown toward the bottom. Hence bidders generally prefer the highest position most and the lowest one the least. In short, the position auction is a multi-object auction where the objects (positions) can be ranked in terms of value from highest (top-most) to lowest (bottom). Although having several different objects complicates matters, because advertisers are restricted to one bid per keyword things simplify. The positions are awarded to the bidders tendering the highest bid and ordered such that the highest bid receives the top, most-preferred spot, and the lowest winning bid receives the bottom position.

The pricing rule used at online ad auctions is typically referred to as a *generalized second-price* (GSP) procedure. The GSP auction is a sealed-bid format where the firm responsible for the ad clicked then pays the next-highest bid—the amount tendered by the advertiser in the position below its own ad; if bids that exceed that of the advertiser successful in luring you to its site are disregarded, the price paid is the second-highest remaining bid. Thus the

Under the auction format used, for each search, the right to a consumer's attention is awarded to the firms willing to pay the most for the opportunity.

payment made by a successful advertiser corresponds to the minimum amount that would be needed to retain its position. Payment for the last position is determined by the bid of the first omitted advertiser, or a minimum reserve price. Although the successful bidders at sponsored search auctions are the firms who tendered the highest bids, payment is only made by an advertiser when someone actually clicks on the ad.

Even though we focused on multi-unit auctions in chapter 7, we noted that much of the discussion could be extended to the case when multiple distinct objects are for sale. The generalized Vickrey auction we investigated can accommodate nonidentical objects, in which case it is referred to as a *Vickrey–Clarke–Groves* (VCG) auction. At a VCG auction, prices still reflect the externality that a given bidder exerts on the pool of auction participants and it remains a weakly dominant strategy for bidders to behave honestly and to bid their valuations, in which case the outcome at auction is also efficient.

The GSP auction resembles the VCG mechanism in that payments are based on the bids tendered by rival bidders—a firm's own bid simply determines the position it is awarded. In fact, with only one advertising slot, the GSP and VCG auctions are equivalent. When several positions exist, the equivalence breaks down because the pricing rules are different. The GSP price equals the next-highest bid, while the VCG price involves the total externality that the winner imposes on rival bidders by taking away an advertising slot and bumping the advertisers that are outbid down a slot (in which case one advertiser also becomes unsuccessful in serving an ad). The pricing rules alter the incentives for bidders; as such, under the GSP pricing rule, truth-telling is typically no longer an equilibrium strategy.

To see how bid shading can be beneficial, modify the example with Alice, Bob, and Charles from the previous chapter. Suppose that there are two positions at auction and the value per click of an ad is $12 for Alice, $9 for Bob, and $7 for Charles. Imagine that the number of expected clicks an ad receives is based only on the position of the ad: no ad-specific effect exists. Specifically, suppose that the most attractive position expects 100 clicks per hour, while the other position expects 75 clicks per hour, regardless of which ad inhabits the position. First, calculate Alice's expected payoff when she and her rivals bid truthfully. In that case Alice wins the top position and pays $9 each time her ad is clicked. Thus she expects to earn ($12 − $9) = $3 per click or $300 given 100 clicks are generated by the top spot. Next, as an alternative, if Bob and Charles bid honestly, but Alice tenders a bid of $8 instead, what will be her expected payoff? In that case she would win the second-best position, given that Bob now outbids her, but she still outbids Charles. The good news is she will pay less for her spot as the price is set by Charles' bid of $7; the bad news is she expects fewer clicks per hour. In this case the good news outweighs the bad because she earns ($12 − $7) = $5 per click, yielding her an expected payoff of $375 as 75 clicks are expected from this ad position. Of course, $375 is greater than $300, so truthful bidding cannot be optimal.

At sponsored search auctions, bidders can change their bids frequently; that is, they can experiment and thus potentially learn about the values of rivals. Moreover Google provides lots of data and offers a Traffic Estimator tool that predicts the number of clicks per day and estimates the cost per day based on keywords. Thus it is not unreasonable to assume that valuations are common knowledge. In other words, complete information exists. Within this setting, *locally envy-free* equilibria have been the focus. At these equilibria no advertiser wants to trade positions with neighboring advertisers—those firms that hold the spots above and below its position. By focusing on these allocations, you can see a relationship between the VCG and GSP auctions. If each bidder submits a tender that the next-highest bidder would have paid in the truth-telling equilibrium of the VCG auction (adjusted for the number of clicks that position generates), then the collection of these strategies constitutes a locally envy-free equilibrium. Moreover this equilibrium corresponds to the worst locally envy-free equilibrium for the search engine and the best for the advertisers. This means that the revenues garnered by the search engine in any locally envy-free equilibrium of the GSP auction are always at least as high as the truth-telling outcome of the VCG auction.

Most important, under the VCG auction, the potential numbers of combinations that would need to be evaluated every time a search query is returned can become prohibitively large—it would simply take too long; the latencies would be unacceptable. The GSP auction circumvents these calculations, so it can be implemented at scale, algorithmically on a computer.

In practice, bids alone do not determine the positions advertisers win: the numbers of clicks are important as well. To compute expected revenues, the search engine must multiply the bid (price-per-click) by the expected number of clicks the hosting site expects the ad to receive. Click-through rates (CTRs) capture the fact that ads have different probabilities of being clicked, even when placed in the same position. Many search engines in fact use complex formulas to weight the bids by some kind of quality score—perhaps a function of CTRs, "relevance" measures given the text being searched for, and whether the ad will provide a positive experience so as to increase your propensity to click ads in the future (that is, some measure of the quality of the advertiser's website).

Display Advertising Auctions

Visiting most websites typically involves being exposed to advertising—be it pop-up ads, article-like ads, or blaring

Adobe Flash ads. Often, such ads are relevant to your lifestyle; sometimes you are even tempted to click. For example, consider visiting the Dictionary.com website. In addition to being able to search the dictionary, you are presented with ads. Such ads may involve animations or other interactive graphics before settling down to the stationary images depicted. On a recent visit we encountered a banner ad for flights on British Airways and two other rectangular ads, one for *Cricket* (a children's magazine), the other for Penske (a moving-truck rental company). Although these may seem unrelated, each ad was in fact quite relevant: the browser used for the Dictionary.com visit had recently been used to book a flight to the United Kingdom, to purchase children's books through various online retailers, and to request price quotations for moving trucks from, among others, Penske. Equipped with such background knowledge, the ads displayed now seem extremely well suited.

Context plays a vital role in online advertising because users accumulate cookies when surfing the web; these cookies can provide an incredibly reliable profile of users. In this sense, advertising has changed dramatically from the static world of *Mad Men* to a dynamic marketplace in which ads can be targeted to consumers with specific tastes. As an example, consider flipping through pages of *The New Yorker* magazine, which contain many pages of ads in addition to the content that typically interests readers. What type of ads do you expect to find in the magazine? Companies that advertise in *The New Yorker* ask a converse question: what type of person reads this magazine? Probably someone educated—who is interested in culture, literature, and news as well as droll cartoons. Because the magazine also announces upcoming events in New York City, readers are more likely from New York than from Dubuque. Because changing copy is costly, the magazine can be printed only a few times. Thus ads for different regions of the country are mostly impossible. Will the reader be female, or male? Of course, experts working within the company are paid to understand who *The New Yorker*'s readers are, so that the magazine can appeal to advertisers. Despite this, what such experts can speculate about readers pales in comparison to what can be understood about web users.

When you visit a website, a variety of information is already known; for example, the operating system of the device as well as the web browser being used. Moreover the Internet protocol (IP) address of your Internet service provider yields fairly accurate information concerning your location. In addition, how you landed on the website can be tracked as well. These attributes, along with the content of the page you are visiting, provide basic information concerning your *type*.

But the real gold is in the cookies—small pieces of data sent from a website and stored in your web browser to remember activity. These cookies paint a revealing picture of who you are as a person—describing your online habits, such as where you get your news, where you shop, which sports teams you like, which music you download, where you went to college, your Facebook likes, perhaps even your political preferences. Armed with this information, advertisers can specify narrow rules for when they might like to advertise and how much they would be willing to pay to do so. By tailoring the conditions of advertising opportunities, firms are willing to pay more relative to the traditional case in which ads are shown to a broad array of consumers. Auctions are helpful in identifying which organizations are interested in and ultimately willing to pay the most for a glimpse from the user's eyes.

For example, a firm might specify what it is willing to pay to place an ad on a website visited by a female, recent college graduate who is currently an unemployed Democrat living in the Bay Area with a penchant for Beyoncé and coffee. Which companies might be interested in attracting this user's attention? Monster.com? *Slate* magazine? Starbucks? Clearly, firms are interested in communicating with individuals who are going to be receptive. Victoria's Secret would be willing to pay a lot more for the opportunity to advertise to this young woman than it would be to a retired man who has no partner. Auctions play the role of discovering which firms are interested in an advertising opportunity and how much they are willing to pay for a perishable good: think about how quickly you surf from one page to a next and whether you wait for ads to load. Along with price discovery, auctions also allocate these opportunities in a fast, fair, and reliable way.

Above, we noted that bids are often transformed using CTRs, or more complex quality scores, so that functions of bids are actually used to allocate advertising opportunities. Another complication, especially for display advertising auctions, involves the different ways in which bids can be submitted and evaluated—for example, some bids are submitted by an ad exchange, a broker between advertisers and publishers. With sponsored search auctions, we employed something referred to as the *cost-per-click* (CPC) or *pay-per-click* pricing: advertisers win slots based on their bids, but payments are only made to the search engine (or publisher) when someone actually clicks on the ad. This means an ad can be served many times before the advertiser actually pays money.

When an ad is shown once, this is referred to as an *impression*. An alternative pricing rule is referred to as *cost-per-mille* (CPM), which is the price an advertiser pays per 1,000 impressions where *mille* is the Latin word for thousand. Less uncertainty exists for the publisher under CPM pricing relative to CPC pricing. Under CPM pricing, advertising is inventory, while under CPC pricing, revenue is determined by the performance of the ad. Under CPM pricing, the publisher is paid each time an impression is served, while under CPC pricing, an action is required of the user. Clearly, CPC pricing requires the seller to think about CTRs and other factors mentioned above, whereas CPM pricing means that bids can simply be ranked from highest to lowest. Finally, even more extreme actions might need to be taken by the user in order for payment to be made—for example, in addition to clicking on the ad, you must complete a form or purchase something on the advertising firm's site. If payment is conditional on post-click behavior, then the pricing structure is referred to as *cost-per-action* (CPA) or *pay-per-action*.

Although advertisers and publishers may have preferences over the various pricing structures, the different payment schemes present challenges. Advertisers affiliated with Google's AdWords looking for display opportunities on Google's Ad Exchange bid primarily on a CPC basis, but auctions on Ad Exchange are typically conducted via CPM pricing. As such, CPM bids must be converted from CPC tenders, which means that the user-response rates must be estimated when constructing expected CPMs. Estimating CPMs can be difficult when the content provider is small or if the queried phrases occur infrequently.

Among the different pricing schemes, which one earns the most? By this point you have probably learned that it depends. CPM pricing shifts revenue risk to the advertisers—the publisher need just serve impressions. In contrast, CPC pricing shifts revenue risk to the publisher. If publishers receive a portion of the advertising revenue, then won't publishers have an incentive to click ads anonymously to pump payments under CPC pricing? Perhaps then, CPA pricing can be used to mitigate fraudulent or dishonest behavior on the part of the publisher. In fact in 2007 Google declared CPA pricing to be the "Holy Grail" of auction-based pricing schemes.

Unfortunately, CPA pricing can have problems as well: a user can take several actions when visiting a website. For example, imagine clicking an ad and then buying one of a number of items offered by an online retailer. Thus advertisers' bids across the possible actions must somehow be consolidated to allow for comparison across firms vying for ad space. Consider summing the product of the probability of an action and the bid for that action over all actions. This aggregation results in a scoring auction. At scoring auctions, bidders can engage in bid skewing: the publisher must estimate probabilities of the various actions in determining a winning bidder. If those probabilities differ from what an advertiser believes, then the advertiser can overbid on actions overestimated by the publisher to increase its chances of winning without really bearing any cost. This problem is compounded when the advertiser is responsible for reporting how frequently actions occur and has control over the site visited. An advertiser may misreport outcomes and manipulate or even prevent certain actions (for example, destroy links), allowing nonserious bids for those actions to win advertising opportunities. Of course, this can generate inefficiencies which derive from the asymmetry in the estimated probabilities of actions between the publisher (or ad exchange depending on the situation) and the advertiser. That is, differing estimates can allow for advertisers with lower valuations to outbid those with higher valuations.

The auctions we first considered in this book were ancient, some of them thousands of years old. In contrast, online ad auctions are just a decade old. The GSP is a new auction format, so researchers are still in the early stages of understanding its properties, let alone accounting for the subtle, but complex incentives that arise in online settings.

REFLECTIONS

In writing this book, we had several goals. First, we hoped to provide readers some notion of how economists think about auctions. We viewed auctions as games of incomplete information where the rules can be used to put structure on real-world behavior that translates into concise, tractable models. Second, the models developed provide a lens through which to understand how incentives affect behavior and often generate clear predictions that can be investigated empirically. In short, we hope you can understand the world better using these models. Finally, and most important, we hoped to provide you with an appreciation for the important role that auctions play in society.

Auctions are used in many situations beyond what we have described because they are flexible ways to discover prices transparently. Successful auction design must accommodate the idiosyncrasies of the market under consideration, which makes it difficult to provide general results but opens the door to bespoke policy advice. Businesses and governments regularly hire auction researchers to provide advice on how to bid at existing auctions and guidance in the design of new ones. Top economists, nearly all of whom are recognized researchers of auctions, now work at eBay, Yahoo!, Google, Amazon, and Microsoft. The government hired leading auctions experts to design its spectrum auctions and bidding firms often employ PhD economists with auction-focused dissertations and research agendas.

In 1998 the US Patent and Trademark Office (USPTO) began awarding patents for the development of new business methods, something previously thought to be too abstract. USPTO class 705 concerns cost/price determination and includes a subclass for developments in the "distribution of services or products ... by an 'auction' or bidding system." All of these opportunities have allowed researchers who study auctions to reach beyond academic audiences and see how well their models hold up in the real world.

Such interactions are not just one sided: often these institutions are willing to use their marketplaces or services as laboratories so that economists can conduct field experiments to evaluate the impact of various policy changes. In these settings an organization might test-drive different policies and alternative rules online, allowing researchers to investigate how consumers, who are unaware that they are involved in a trial, respond. This collaboration between the ivory tower and the major players in today's economy ensures that auctions will remain crucial to the marketplace in the future.

If anything, our discussion understates the role auctions play in our society. For example, we have assumed explicitly that just one seller (or, in the case of a procurement auction, one buyer) exists, so we have ignored the effect of other participants. In general, however, both sides of the market may participate—often referred to as a *double auction*. At double auctions, several (perhaps many) buyers and sellers jointly submit bids to buy and to sell, which then determines market prices. In 1792 John Sutton and other financial leaders gathered in Manhattan at 22 Wall Street to sell securities at auction each day. This was, of course, the precursor of the New York Stock Exchange. Prices are also determined at auction on the Chicago Board of Trade. Although these markets typically involve larger numbers of buyers and sellers (more than the few we had in mind), many of the incentives we have highlighted apply to these environments as well.

As this example illustrates, naturally, page constraints limit the number of modifications to the auction rules and descriptions of complications that might arise in certain real-world auctions that we could delve into. As we alluded to, the settings in which auctions can be used and the pricing rules that can be specified are only limited by the imagination of the auction designer. Nonetheless, we hope you have enjoyed the ride. We sought to equip you not only with an understanding of how auctions work, and an appreciation of the roles auctions play in our society but also with some intuition about the fundamental trade-offs at play. We deliberately chose certain models: once you understand how they work, you can apply these ideas to settings beyond those described.

For example, when firms win the right to drill for oil, they not only pay their bids (actually referred to as the *bonus* payment), they must often also pay royalties on any oil extracted. The royalty payments usually correspond to a fixed fraction of revenues the drilling firm earns. Why might these auctions be structured in this way? Given immense randomness that is oil exploration, royalty payments allow the government and interested firms to share risks. Perhaps you can see how such risk sharing might allow bidders to be more comfortable in bidding competitively at these auctions.

We have been silent on constraints such as budgets or capacities, but such constraints are a reality: firms have limited capital; team owners in fantasy football drafts have limited funds. When bidders face differential constraints, asymmetries arise, which you know can be important in generating differences in the strategies bidders employ. As such, inefficiencies can arise—perhaps you can use that as an explanation for why you might have failed to acquire Andrew Luck in a draft auction. Constraints can be a nice way of extending the models we've considered to dynamic settings in which winning something today affects your ability to bid tomorrow. In dynamic models the option of bidding tomorrow has value that must be internalized by decision makers in current periods.

Although we did not explicitly involve psychological factors in our discussions, these surely play an important role in practice. A list of employees who were diverted from concentration camps, drawn up by Oskar Schindler, was put up for auction on eBay, but received no bids—perhaps because the reserve price of $3 million reflected some sentimental value to a descendant of Itzak Stern (Schindler's accountant). Regardless of how much the seller values the object, as we saw, an optimal reserve price exceeds the seller's valuation. Behavioral economists have employed the models we've presented in accommodating ideas from psychology to see how cognitive and emotional factors affect how people bid at auctions. Certain auction formats and pricing rules generate excitement and thus do a better job of fostering bidding wars among competitors than others. Competition is essential to the success of an auction, so open formats could be helpful in encouraging such behavior. As we now know, the price a seller expects to receive increases with the number of participants at an auction. As such, designing auctions to attract as many bidders as possible should always be a consideration.

In our discussions of multi-unit and multi-object auctions, we suggested that many complications can arise. For example, in some cases the value of a bundle of objects is worth more than the sum of the value of each individually. Package bidding makes sense when the objects at auction should not be considered separately, perhaps because the objects are complementary to one another, or when some set of the objects might be used instead of another. Referred to as *combinatorial auctions*, these mechanisms are used to sell everything from arrival and departure slots at LaGuardia Airport to allocating the electromagnetic spectrum in some countries. Such interactions generate challenges. As with the VCG auction, it can become computationally impractical to determine the winning bidder in some settings. It should be no surprise then that bidders can be confused about how to begin thinking about behavior for complex pricing rules. Researchers are thus working to construct pricing rules so that bidders have a simple strategy: tell the truth. Our investigation of the single-object second-price auctions, the GVA, the Ausubel auction and the VCG auction allow you to understand how such design is possible.

Although a reputable, trusted legal system is central to all market-based economies, in order for auctions to work well, trust is required. Sellers dissatisfied with the outcome of an auction cannot deviate from the prescribed rules; buyers need to fulfill the bids made at auctions. In *Adarand v. Peña* (1995) the US Supreme Court ruled that the right to favor certain groups of bidders (or subcontractors) over others must be considered under a level of "strict scrutiny." Because minority subcontracting goals and bidder preferences are contentious, some states have sought alternatives, such as bidder-training programs. In other situations ethical questions can arise. For instance, in January 2014 the Dallas Safari Club sold the right to hunt a male black rhinoceros in Namibia, despite black rhinos being considered a "critically endangered species." A well-functioning legal system and an understanding of the incentives at play are important to keeping in check the ambitions of sellers and, as we saw in our discussion of collusion, the buyers.

We hope this introduction to auctions allows you to think creatively—be it in recognizing situations in the real world that share common features or generate similar incentives to auctions or in applying auctions in novel ways. If you're a regular bidder at auctions, we hope you recognize the need to internalize rivals' potential strategies when considering how you should behave. If you participate as a seller or can influence policy-making, we hope you understand the trade-offs the various auction formats involve and see how optimal auction design can involve different prescriptions for different environments. Regardless, we appreciate your taking the time to learn about auctions and hope our presentation sparks for you the same curiosity and appreciation for auctions that we maintain.

Affiliated values

Valuations of bidders for the object at auction that are dependent in a special way, statistically; for example, because of a common component (with unknown value) as well as an idiosyncratic component that is private information. In the affiliated private-values paradigm, payoffs do not depend on the common component, but valuations are still positively dependent.

All-pay auction

An auction at which every bidder who submits a positive tender (including those who lose the auction) must make some payment.

Ausubel auction

An open-format version of the generalized Vickrey auction at which the price rises and bidders report how many units they would like to purchase. As units are allocated, prices at which rivals drop out are recorded and reflect the payments that will be required of bidders winning various units.

Bayes–Nash equilibrium

A collection of strategies, one for each player, such that the expected payoff to each player is maximized given the strategies played by rivals and players' beliefs about their rivals' types.

Best response

A strategy that provides the highest payoff to a player given the player's beliefs about what rivals will do.

Collusion

An attempt by bidders, either overtly or tacitly, to limit competition, often by cooperating with each other for their mutual benefit.

Common knowledge

Notion that all players know and understand the game's structure and rules, everyone knows that all players know these things, everyone knows everyone knows everyone knows these things, *ad infinitum*.

Common value

Object at auction (like a jar of coins) has the same value to participants, but this value is unknown to all participants and only revealed after the auction. Bidders have different estimates of the object's true value, which leads to different bids in equilibrium.

Complete information

A game where the identities of the players, the feasible strategies available to each player, and the preferences of all players, as reflected by the potential payoffs to each player for every possible outcome, are common knowledge.

Cost-per-action (CPA) pricing

Bidders win advertising opportunities based on their bids, but payment is only made when someone actually clicks on the ad and takes some action afterward, such as completing a form or making a purchase from the advertiser.

Cost-per-click (CPC) pricing

Bidders win advertising opportunities based on their bids, but payment is only made when someone actually clicks on the ad.

Cost-per-mille (CPM) pricing

Bidders win advertising opportunities based on their bids and payment is made to the publisher for the right to serve 1,000 impressions.

Discriminatory auction

A multi-object auction at which the pricing rule dictates that the bidders tendering the most for the objects be awarded the objects and each pay the amounts they bid.

Display advertising auction

An auction for the right to serve advertisements on regular websites in which context plays a crucial role; advertisers' requests can be highly tailored to the setting and characteristics of the user.

Dominant strategy

A strategy that maximizes payoffs for a player for all possible actions rivals may take. If the payoffs are strictly higher for all combinations of rivals' actions, the strategy is a strictly dominant strategy; if payoffs are at least as great as what a player might earn by doing something else and strictly greater for at least one possibility, the strategy is a weakly dominant strategy.

Dutch auction
An open-format auction at which the asking price is lowered until a bidder indicates she/he is willing to pay the amount being asked; that bidder is declared the winner and must pay the price that stopped the auction; sometimes referred to as an *oral, descending-price auction*.

Efficiency
An auction is efficient if it ensures that the player (buyer or seller) valuing the item the most is allocated the item at the end of the auction.

English auction
An open-format auction at which price increases until just one bidder (the winner) remains; the winner pays the price that induced the last rival bidder to exit the auction; sometimes referred to as an *oral, ascending-price auction*.

First-price auction
An auction at which the pricing rule dictates that the highest bidder pay the amount that bidder tendered for the object at auction; sometimes referred to as a *pay-your-bid auction*.

Generalized second-price (GSP) auction
A sealed-bid auction used for sponsored-search and display auctions at which the pricing rule requires winning bidders to pay the amount of the next-highest bid, often only when users click on an advertisement.

Generalized Vickrey auction (GVA)
A multi-unit auction at which sealed bids are solicited. The highest bidders are awarded the units. Prices for each unit won correspond with the amount the bidder who is displaced (would have won the unit had the winner not participated) was willing to pay for that unit. When several heterogeneous objects are at auction and such a pricing rule and format is used, we refer to this as a *Vickrey–Clarke–Groves (VCG) auction*.

Incomplete information

Some aspect of the game is not common knowledge. In auction games, typically the exact private valuations of rivals, or their estimates of the common value for the object at auction, are private information. As such the payoffs to each player for a given outcome are unknown by the seller and rival bidders.

Independent private values (IPV)

Bidders have private valuations for the object at auction that are independent from each other. Valuations are private information and learning one bidder's valuation does not change other bidders' valuations.

Nash equilibrium

A collection of strategies, one for each player, such that the payoff to each player is maximized given the strategies played by rivals.

Open-format auction

An auction at which price evolves in a way that is publicly-observed by all bidders.

Pay-your-bid auction

A first-price, sealed-bid auction at which the highest bidder is declared the winner and pays the amount tendered.

Procurement auction

A situation in which a sole buyer (monopsonist) solicits sealed-bid tenders from bidders (typically firms) indicating the amounts they would require to be paid in order to complete some task for the buyer. The buyer awards the contract to the bidder tendering the lowest amount and pays the bidder the amount the bidder requested. Also referred to as a *reverse* or *low-price, sealed-bid auction*.

Proxy bid

An automated way to bid where bidders report the highest price they would be willing to pay to a system that bids on their behalf by entering the minimum amount necessary to overtake other bidders, so long as the maximum price entered by the bidder exceeds the current asking price.

Reserve price

Minimum amount that a seller is willing to accept for an object at auction. Reserve prices may be announced before an auction is conducted or kept secret until the conclusion of an auction.

Revenue equivalence theorem

A result that says expected revenues to the seller will be the same for any auction that allocates the object efficiently and ensures bidders with the lowest possible type get zero expected payoffs, so long as bidders are risk neutral and valuations are drawn independently and identically from a continuous distribution.

Scoring auction

An auction at which a formal rule is announced that combines monetary bids with other attributes of an offer (such as time to completion or quality of materials being used in a procurement setting) to determine a winner.

Sealed-bid auction

A closed-format auction at which tenders are privately submitted by bidders; the bid of any participant is unknown to rivals.

Second-price auction

An auction at which the pricing rule dictates that the highest bidder pay the amount tendered by the second-highest bidder.

Shill bid

A nonserious bid intended merely to drive up the price at which the object at auction is sold.

Sniping

When an auction is set to end at a fixed time and a bidder waits until the final seconds to submit a bid that exceeds the current posted price, leaving rivals little to no time to respond.

Sponsored search auction

An auction conducted for the right to serve ads alongside organic search results returned from search engines. Also referred to as a *position* or *keywords* auction.

Strategy
A rule prescribing a feasible action for every possible type a player might be. In models of auctions, a strategy typically conveys the amount a player should tender for every possible valuation the player might have.

Type
A player's private information, determined by Nature. At auctions, a player's type is typically her or his private valuation or estimate of the common value for the object at auction.

Uniform-price auction
A multi-unit auction at which the pricing rule involves all winning bidders paying the same price, typically the highest losing bid (or sometimes the lowest winning bid). The winners are those bidders who tendered more than (at least as much as) the requisite amount.

Valuation
A bidder's type: the private information representing the most the bidder would be willing to pay for the object at auction.

Vickrey auction
A second-price, sealed-bid auction. We use the term to refer to auctions at which a single object is being sold; see *generalized Vickrey auction* for insight into a multi-unit setting.

Winner-pay auction
An auction at which only the winning bidder is required to make payment as determined by the pricing rule.

Winner's curse
A situation, typically at common-value auctions, where the winning bidder is in some sense disappointed by winning as it indicates she/he had the most optimistic impression of the item at auction and, by winning, learns that she/he might have overpaid.

FURTHER READING

For those interested in reading more about auctions, a vast literature exists. By and large, as was mentioned in the preface, this literature can often be quite technical mathematically, but the hard work is rewarding. The first four papers are surveys that go beyond our gentle introduction; the next eight books go well beyond the surveys.

Survey Articles

Klemperer, Paul. 1999. Auction theory: A guide to the literature. *Journal of Economic Surveys* 13: 227–286.

McAfee, R. Preston, and John McMillan. 1987. Auctions and bidding. *Journal of Economic Literature* 25: 699–738.

Milgrom, Paul. 1989. Auctions and bidding: A primer. *Journal of Economic Perspectives* 3: 3–22.

Wolfsetter, Elmar. 1996. Auctions: An introduction. *Journal of Economic Surveys* 10: –420.

Book-Length Treatments

Cassady, Ralph Jr. 1967. *Auctions and Auctioneering*. Berkeley: University of California Press.

Cramton, Peter, Yoav Shoham, and Richard Steinberg, eds. 2006. *Combinatorial Auctions*. Cambridge: MIT Press.

Klemperer, Paul D. 2004. *Auctions: Theory and Practice*. Princeton: Princeton University Press.

Krishna, Vijay. 2010. *Auction Theory*, 2nd ed. San Diego: Academic Press.

Menezes, Flavio M., and Paulo K. Monteiro. 2004. *An Introduction to Auction Theory*. New York: Oxford University Press.

Milgrom, Paul R. 2004. *Putting Auction Theory to Work*. New York: Cambridge University Press.

Paarsch, Harry J., and Han Hong. 2006. *An Introduction to the Structural Econometrics of Auction Data*. Cambridge: MIT Press.

Steiglitz, Kenneth. 2007. *Snipers, Shills, and Sharks: eBay and Human Behavior*. Princeton: Princeton University Press.

BIBLIOGRAPHY

These papers and texts helped inform our discussion. Although we avoided in-text citations (to promote continuity), we should like to acknowledge the work that formed the basis of our arguments.

Agarwal, Nikhil, Susan Athey, and David Yang. 2009. Skewed bidding in pay-per-action auctions for online advertising. *American Economic Review* 99: 441–47.

Asker, John, and Estelle Cantillon. 2008. Properties of scoring auctions. *RAND Journal of Economics* 39: 69–85.

Asker, John, and Estelle Cantillon. 2010. Procurement when price and quality matter. *RAND Journal of Economics* 41: 1–34.

Athey, Susan, and Jonathan Levin. 2001. Information and competition in US Forest Service timber auctions. *Journal of Political Economy* 109: 375–417.

Ausubel, Lawrence M. 2004. An efficient ascending-bid auction for multiple objects. *American Economic Review* 94: 1452–75.

Ausubel, Lawrence M., Peter Cramton, Marek Pycia, Marzena Rostek, and Marek Weretka. 2014. Demand reduction and inefficiency in multi-unit auctions. *Review of Economic Studies* 81: 1366–1400.

Bax, Eric, Anand Kuratti, Preston McAfee, and Julian Romero. 2012. Comparing predicted prices in auctions for online advertising. *International Journal of Industrial Organization* 30: 80–88.

Cabral, Luis, and Ali Hortaçsu. 2010. The dynamics of seller reputation: Evidence from eBay. *Journal of Industrial Economics* 58: 54–78.

Carpenter, Jeffrey, Jessica Holmes, and Peter Hans Matthews. 2014. "Bucket auctions" for charity. *Games and Economic Behavior* 88: 260–76.

Cramton, Peter, and Jesse A. Schwartz. 2002. Collusive bidding in the FCC spectrum auctions. *Contributions to Economic Analysis and Policy* 1: 1–18.

Decarolis, Francesco. 2014. Awarding price, contract performance, and bids screening: Evidence from procurement auctions. *American Economic Journal: Applied Economics* 6: 108–32.

Edelman, Benjamin, Michael Ostrovsky, and Michael Schwarz. 2007. Internet advertising and the generalized second-price auction: Selling billions of dollars' worth of keywords. *American Economic Review* 97: 242–59.

Einav, Liran, Chiara Farronato, Jonathan D. Levin, and Neel Sundaresan. 2013. Sales mechanisms in online markets: What happened to Internet auctions? Working paper 19021. NBER.

Elyakime, Bernard, Jean Jacques Laffont, Patrice Loisel, and Quang Vuong. 1994. First-price sealed-bid auctions with secret reservation prices. *Annales d'Économie et de Statistique* 34: 115–41.

Engelberg, Joseph, and Jared Williams. 2009. eBay's proxy bidding: A license to shill. *Journal of Economic Behavior and Organization* 72: 509–526.

Friedman, James W. 1971. A non-cooperative equilibrium for supergames. *Review of Economic Studies* 38: 1–12.

Graham, Daniel A., and Robert C. Marshall. 1987. Collusive bidder behavior at single-object second-price and English auctions. *Journal of Political Economy* 95: 1217–39.

Harsanyi, John C. 1967–88. Games of incomplete information played by "Bayesian" players, parts I–III. *Management Science* 14: 159–82, 320–34, and 486–502.

Hickman, Brent R., Timothy P. Hubbard, and Harry J. Paarsch. 2014. Investigating the economic importance of pricing-rule mis-specification in empirical models of electronic auctions. Working paper. University of Chicago.

Hubbard, Timothy P., and Harry J. Paarsch. 2009. Investigating bid preferences at low-price, sealed-bid auctions with endogenous participation. *International Journal of Industrial Organization* 27: 1–14.

Jin, Ginger Zhe, and Andrew Kato. 2006. Price, quality, and reputation: Evidence from an online field experiment. *RAND Journal of Economics* 37: 983–1005.

Kagel, John H., and Dan Levin. 1986. The winner's curse and public information in common value auctions. *American Economic Review* 76: 894–920.

Klemperer, Paul. 1999. Auction theory: A guide to the literature. *Journal of Economic Surveys* 13: 227–86.

Klemperer, Paul D. 2004. *Auctions: Theory and Practice*. Princeton: Princeton University Press.

Krishna, Vijay. 2002. *Auction Theory*. San Diego: Academic Press.

Krishna, Vijay. 2010. *Auction Theory*, 2nd ed. San Diego: Academic Press.

Krishna, Vijay, and Motty Perry. 2000. Efficient mechanism design. Working paper. Penn State University.

Li, Tong, and Xiaoyong Zheng. 2009. Entry and competition effects in first-price auctions: Theory and evidence from procurement auctions. *Review of Economic Studies* 76: 1397–1429.

McAfee, R. Preston, and John McMillan. 1987. Auctions and bidding. *Journal of Economic Literature* 25: 699–738.

McDonald, Cynthia G., and V. Carlos Slawson, Jr. 2002. Reputation in an Internet auction market. *Economic Inquiry* 40: 633–50.

McMillan, John. 1994. Selling spectrum rights. *Journal of Economic Perspectives* 8: 145–62.

Milgrom, Paul. 1989. Auctions and bidding: A primer. *Journal of Economic Perspectives* 3: 3–22.

Milgrom, Paul R. 2004. *Putting Auction Theory to Work*. New York: Cambridge University Press.

Milgrom, Paul R., and Robert J. Weber. 1982. A theory of auctions and competitive bidding. *Econometrica* 50: 1089–1122.

Myerson, Roger B. 1981. Optimal auction design. *Mathematics of Operations Research* 6: 55–73.

Nash, John. 1951. Non-cooperative games. *Annals of Mathematics* 54: 286–95.

Porter, Robert H., and J. Douglas Zona. 1993. Detection of bid rigging in procurement auctions. *Journal of Political Economy* 101: 518–38.

Riley, John G., and William F. Samuelson. Optimal auctions. 1981. *American Economic Review* 71: 381–92.

Roberts, James W. 2011. Can warranties substitute for reputations? *American Economic Journal: Microeconomics* 3: 69–85.

Roth, Alvin E., and Axel Ockenfels. 2002. Last-minute bidding and the rules for ending second-price auctions: Evidence from eBay and Amazon auctions on the Internet. *American Economic Review* 92: 1093–1103.

Steiglitz, Kenneth. 2007. *Snipers, Shills, and Sharks: eBay and Human Behavior*. Princeton: Princeton University Press.

Varian, Hal R. 2007. Position auctions. *International Journal of Industrial Organization* 25: 1163–1178.

Vickrey, William. 1961. Counterspeculation, auctions and competitive sealed tenders. *Journal of Finance* 16: 8–37.

Wilson, Robert B. 1977. A bidding model of perfect competition. *Review of Economic Studies* 44: 511–18.

Wolfsetter, Elmar. 1996. Auctions: An introduction. *Journal of Economic Surveys* 10: 367–420.

INDEX

Wu-Tang Clan, 3

TIMOTHY P. HUBBARD is Assistant Professor of Economics at Colby College. After initial appointments at the University of British Columbia and the University of Western Ontario, HARRY J. PAARSCH held the position of Professor of Economics and Robert Jensen Research Fellow in the Henry B. Tippie College of Business at the University of Iowa and subsequently Chair in Economics at the University of Melbourne. From 2011 to 2014 he worked as an applied economist and data scientist for Amazon.com.